WALKING WITH GOD
STUDY GUIDE

OTHER BOOKS BY JOHN ELDREDGE

Beautiful Outlaw

Captivating (with Stasi Eldredge)

Epic

Fathered by God

Free to Live

Killing Lions (with Sam Eldredge)

Knowing the Heart of God

Love and War (with Stasi Eldredge)

Moving Mountains

The Sacred Romance (with Brent Curtis)

Waking the Dead

Walking with God

Wild at Heart

WALKING WITH GOD
STUDY GUIDE

HOW TO HEAR HIS VOICE

JOHN ELDREDGE
with CRAIG McCONNELL

Harper*Christian*
Resources

Walking with God Study Guide
© 2008 and 2017 by John Eldredge

Requests for information should be addressed to:
HarperChristian Resources, 3900 Sparks Dr. SE, Grand Rapids, Michigan 49546

ISBN 978-0-310-08477-8 (softcover)
ISBN 978-0-310-08478-5 (ebook)

HarperChristian Resources titles may be purchased in bulk for church, business, fundraising, or ministry use. For information, please e-mail ResourceSpecialist@ChurchSource.com.

First Printing January 2017 / Printed in the United States of America

Contents

INTRODUCTION

You've made a very good decision, picking up this guide.

For what could be more important, than learning to more closely walk with God?

That's why I wrote the book, and why Craig and I then wrote this guide. Now, I'm assuming you've got a copy of the book *Walking with God* as well. The two go hand in hand. Most of the time I recommend users of my workbooks and guides read through the whole book first. It helps to get your bearings, gives you the lay of the land. But *Walking with God* is different. It unfolds. You *could* read the whole book (you might not be able to put it down!), but you don't have to. For this guide I'd recommend you simply read a section at a time (the sections are Prelude, Summer, Fall, Winter, and Spring). Then go back through and think about it with the help of this guide.

In the Introduction to the book I said this:

> Some of these stories will open up new horizons for you. That is certainly my hope. Learning to hear the voice of God may itself be a new frontier, and an exciting one, with unexpected joys around each new turn. There will also no doubt be lessons you've already learned, probably better than I. But, you may have forgotten. We do forget, even the most precious encounters we have with God. Perhaps I will help you to remember, and recover what

might have been lost. I might also help you to tell your own story as well, give you eyes to see what is unfolding and even how to set it down so that it doesn't slip away (*Walking with God*, pages xii–xiii).

Now, because the whole purpose of the book and guide are to help you find God in your story, learn to listen to his voice, and walk with him more intimately, you will want to write down what unfolds for you. Capture what he says. Don't let it slip away! JOURNAL ALONG THE WAY. Not just your responses to the questions I've provided, but whatever is coming to you as you go along. Especially what you believe God is saying to you.

What is so very cool is that God will seize the opportunity of you working through this guide and he will "coordinate" the events of your life or the things he is trying to teach you with the topics and the stories you'll be reading here. What he'll often do is use the very things I've been writing about from my life as a mirror into your life, in order to take you to some very personal and intimate places with him in your own story. It will be good.

Walking with God is an "interactive" book. I created a website to go along with it, and on that site I offer a lot more explanation and guidance on particular entries in the book. (Those are marked with a reference to www.walkingwithgod.net.) I think you'll find those really helpful, so make sure you drop by the site whenever I refer to it in the book.

Okay, here we go. I'd recommend you read the Prelude to begin with, and then dive into the questions.

Prelude

Learning to Hear the Voice of God

I began the book with the story of our family's Christmas tree ordeal for two reasons. First, to let you see that my life is just like yours. I face hassles all the time, just as you do. Some of them are exasperating, just like yours. But I also wanted to begin with a confession—this ordeal happened because I didn't follow God.

≋ Has something like our tree ordeal happened to you this year? But of course it has. Trials are part of every life. What do you make of them? How do you understand all the hassles that come your way? Pick one that's happened to you. Think about it. Did you ask God about it beforehand? Did you even think to ask?

≋ If you did seek God beforehand, what do you make of the fact that things still fell apart? If you didn't, has it occurred to you that maybe the reason for the trial is that you *didn't* ask?

How many things in an ordinary week of your life *do* you ask God about? (There's no shame here. I'm not asking this to cause you embarrassment or self-reproach. It's just probably a good idea to begin this search for a closer walk with God by admitting where you are.)

Assumptions

Okay. Let's look at assumptions. This is a very good place to dive in. Assumptions govern so much of our lives, or at least, our *interpretation* of our lives.

> I left the store thinking about assumptions—how they are either helping us or hurting us, every single day of our lives. Our assumptions control our interpretation of events, and they supply a great deal of the momentum and direction for our lives. It's important that we take a look at them. And life will provide hundreds of opportunities to take a look at our assumptions in a single week. Especially as we walk with God (*Walking with God*, page 5).

Think of an event in your life where things didn't turn out the way you hoped, or expected. What did you assume about all of it?

As we get set to enter into a closer walk with God, it would be good to note that so much of what God is doing as we go along is surfacing our assumptions, or challenging them, *so that* he can help to set them right. After all, Jesus said when we know the truth we are set free. I talked about my friend at the bookstore, how he held to the assumption that A + B = C.

> He assumed that God, being a loving God, was going to come through for him. In the sense of, bless his choices. His ministry. Make his life good. He looked sort of dazed and hurt that it hadn't happened. He was trying to put a good face on it, but you could see that he had lost heart. This may be one of the most common, most unquestioned, and most naïve assumptions people who believe in God share. We assume that because we believe in God, and because he is love, he's going to give us a happy life. A + B = C. We may not be so bold as to state our assumption out loud—you may not even think you hold this assumption—but notice your shock when things don't go well. Notice your feelings of abandonment and betrayal when life doesn't work out. Notice that often you feel as though God isn't really all that close, or involved, feel that he isn't paying attention to your life (page 4).

Can you relate? Do you recognize it in your life or in the lives of those you know?

It might be good to jot down a few more assumptions you hold about God and life. You might be surprised what you confess. What are you assuming about God these days?

How about God in your life?

And happiness—what do you assume about that?

The reason I'm pushing into that with these questions is, as I wrote, "If you don't hold the same assumptions Jesus does, you haven't got a chance of finding the life he has for you."

DOES GOD STILL SPEAK?

I confessed in the Prelude my assumption that God still speaks, personally, to his people. What do you believe about that?

Seeing as how this book is in part a tutorial on how to hear the voice of God, we'd better pause here and deal with the evidence on which my conviction is based. (I suppose you could still gain a good deal from this book if you don't believe God speaks, but you'll miss a pretty central point.)

Do you believe God speaks to you?

What is your assumption based on?

Reread Psalm 139. How intimately does God know you?

But does God speak to his people?

Can you imagine any relationship where there is no communication whatsoever? What would you think if you met two friends for coffee, good friends, and you knew that they'd been there at the café for an hour before you arrived, and as you sit down you ask them, "So, what have you been talking about?" and they said, "Nothing." "Nothing?" "Nothing. We don't talk to each other. But we're really good friends." Jesus calls us his friends: "I'm no longer calling you servants because servants don't understand what their master is thinking and planning. No, I've named you friends because I've let you in on everything I've heard from the Father" (John 15:15, *The Message*).

Or what would you think about a father if you asked him, "What have you been talking to your children about lately?" and he said, "Nothing. I don't talk to them. But I love them very much." Wouldn't you say the relationship was missing something? And aren't you God's son or daughter? "Yet to all who received him, to those who believed in his name, he gave the right to become children of God" (John 1:12) (pages 10–11).

Well—what about those analogies? You are God's child. You are Jesus' friend. Why would he never speak to you, personally?

The Bible is *filled* with stories of God talking to his people. Abraham, who is called the friend of God, said, "The Lord, the God of heaven, who brought me out of my father's household and my native land and who spoke to me . . . " (Genesis 24:7). God spoke to Moses "as a man speaks with his friend" (Exodus 33:11). He spoke to Aaron, too: "Now the Lord spoke to Moses and Aaron about the Israelites . . ." (Exodus 6:13). And David: "In the course of time, David inquired of the Lord. 'Shall I go up to one of the towns of Judah?' he asked. The Lord said, 'Go up.' David asked, 'Where shall I go?' 'To Hebron,' the Lord answered" (2 Samuel 2:1). The Lord spoke to Noah. The Lord spoke to Gideon. The Lord spoke to Samuel. The list goes on and on. Now, if God doesn't also speak to us, why would he have given us all these stories of him speaking to others? "Look—here are hundreds of inspiring and hopeful stories of how God spoke to his people in this and that situation. Isn't it amazing?! But you can't have that. He doesn't speak like that anymore." That makes no sense at all. Why would God give you a book of exceptions? "This is how I used to relate to my people, but I don't do that anymore." What good would a book of exceptions do you? That's like giving you the owner's manual for a Dodge, even though you drive a Mitsubishi. No, the Bible is a book of examples of what it looks like to walk with God (pages 11–13).

- Have you assumed the Bible, or at least all those stories of God speaking to his people—those are exceptions?

- Why would God give you a book of exceptions?

The Bible teaches that we hear God's voice:

He wakens me morning by morning,
    wakens my ear to listen like one being taught (Isaiah 50:4).

For he is our God
    and we are the people of his pasture,
    the flock under his care. (Psalm 95:7)

Today, if you hear his voice,
    do not harden your hearts . . . (Psalm 95:7–8).

The man who enters by the gate is the shepherd of his sheep. The watchman opens the gate for him, and the sheep listen to his voice. He calls his own sheep by name and leads them out. When he has brought out all his own, he goes on ahead of them, and his sheep follow him because they know his voice . . . I am the good shepherd; I know my sheep and my sheep know me— just as the Father knows me and I know the Father—and I lay down my life for the sheep. I have other sheep that are not of this sheep pen. I must bring them also. They too will listen to my voice, and there shall be one flock and one shepherd (John 10:2–4, 14–16).

Here I am! I stand at the door and knock. If anyone hears my voice and opens the door, I will come in and eat with him, and he with me (Revelation 3:20).

We are his sheep. Jesus says that his sheep hear his voice. He stands and knocks. Who is the offer for? "Anyone." That would include you. What does Jesus say will happen? "Hears my voice."

So there—you have my first assumption. An intimate, con-versational walk with God is available. Is normal, even. Or, at least, is *meant* to be normal. I'm well aware that a majority of people do not enjoy that . . . yet. But it is certainly what God desires, and what he offers. My assumption is based on the nature of God, and the nature of man made in his image. We are communicators. It is based on the nature of relationship—it requires communication. It is based on the long record of God speaking to his people, of various ranks and in all sorts of situa-tions. And it is based on the teachings of Jesus, who tells us that we hear his voice (pages 13–14, 16).

Well—does this help you believe God wants to speak to you, personally, intimately? What would you love to hear from God on? Make a point to gently ask God about that this week. Keep coming back to the question.

What Is God Up To???

I told the story of God stopping me from sending an email that wasn't going to help me or the person I was planning on roasting. The point is this: You'll find it helps a great deal in your following if you know what God is up to.

> True, we may not know *exactly* what God is up to in this or that event in our life. "Why didn't I get the job?" "How come she won't return my calls?" "Why haven't my prayers healed this cancer?" I don't know. Sometimes we can get clarity, and sometimes we can't.
>
> But whatever else is going on, we *can* know this—he is *always* up to our transformation.

> God knew what he was doing from the very beginning. He decided from the outset to shape the lives of those who love him along the same lines as the life of his Son. The Son stands first in the line of humanity he restored. We see the original and intended shape of our lives there in him. After God made that decision of what his children should be like, he followed it up by calling people by name. After he called them by name, he set them on a solid basis with himself. And then, after getting them established, he stayed with them to the end, gloriously completing what he had begun. (Romans 8:29–30, *The Message*)

God has something in mind. He is deeply and personally committed to restoring humanity. Restoring you. There was a man or woman he had in mind when he made you. By bringing you back to himself through the work of Jesus Christ, he has established relationship with you. And now, what he's up to is restoring you. The way that happens is to shape your life "along the same lines as the life of his Son." To shape you into the image of Jesus. You can be confident of this. It's a given. Whatever else might be going on in your life, God always has his eye on your transformation (pages 17–18).

How do you feel about going there—to be transformed?

What might God be after in your life these days—do you have a hunch where transformation is needed, what he might be putting his finger on? Can you name it?

God wants us to be happy. Really. "I have come that they may have life and have it to the full" (John 10:10). But he knows that in order for us to be truly happy, we have to be whole. Another word for that is holy. We have to be restored.

Think of it this way—think of how you feel when you really screw things up. The look on your son's face as you yell at him. The distance that's grown between you, even though you apologized. For the hundredth time. How it tears you up inside to indulge in romantic fantasies about someone else's spouse. You want that but you don't want that but you wish you could but you really don't and why is this going on inside? The guilt you feel when you lie straight-faced to a friend. And they find out. The hours you've wasted harboring resentment. The embarrassment of your addictions. You know what plagues you (page 19).

Now, what would it be like to never, ever do it again? To not even struggle with it. What would your life be like if you were free of all that haunts you?

Summer

A Time of Restoration and Renewal, and for Finding Our Way Back to Joy

Okay, here's what I suggest you do—read the section called Summer in the book, and then come back to this guide and dive into the following reflections.

SLOWING DOWN TO LISTEN

I begin with the story from the first day of my summer vacation, how God pinned me down on the porch of our cabin in order to raise some issues in my life. What struck you about the story, what did you identify with?

> Trapped on the porch, I know the issue is far bigger than this vacation. I know that full well. The issue is the way I live my life. And, forced for a few moments to stop, I also know that I don't want to live like this. The very things I'm doing to try and make life happen—all those things that feel so inevitable and unavoidable—they are draining me, and preventing me from finding the life God offers (*Walking with God*, page 23).

☀ This is an epiphany for most of us. The way we live our lives is actually preventing us from living the life God wants us to live. Because all that we are doing and chasing feels so inevitable. But do you like the pace of your life?

Does your life feel "easy" and "light," as in "my yoke is easy and my burden is light?"

> Now, rest is just one of the ways we receive the life of God. We stop, set it all down, and allow ourselves to be replenished. This is supposed to happen regularly. I think the original prescription was weekly. So why does rest feel like a luxury? Seriously, it feels irresponsible. We think we can drive ourselves like oxen fifty weeks a year, resurrect in a two-week vacation, then go back and do it all again. This is madness. My pushing and striving cuts me off from the life I so desperately need. I don't even think to stop and ask, *Is this what you'd have me do, Lord? Do you want me to paint the bathroom? Volunteer at church? Stay late at work* (page 24)*?*

How often do you stop and rest, truly rest?

I'm back to the shepherd and the sheep—when the sheep follow the shepherd, they find pasture. They find life. The life doesn't just magically come to us.

Pause. Let that sink in. The life doesn't just magically come to us. Prior to reading this book, how *did* you believe the life of God comes to you? I mean, what was your plan to find the life God offers?

How does your current way of life reveal your plan to find life?

We have to make ourselves available to it. There is a lifestyle that allows us to receive the life of God. I know that if I will live more intimately with Jesus, and follow his voice, I've got a much better chance of finding the life I long for. I know it. If I will listen to his voice, and let him set the pace, if I will cooperate in my transformation, I think I would be a much happier man. And so a new prayer has begun to rise within me. I am asking God,

What is the life you want me to live?

If we could get an answer to that question, it would change everything (page 24).

Are you willing to ask that question? Would you be willing to make whatever changes are necessary to live the life God wants you to live?

Are there areas of your life or your plans that you'd rather God not interfere with? Another way of asking this is, what do you fear God will ask you to change if you really let him have your whole way of life?

So go ahead—ask him. Right now. What is the life you want me to live? Listen for a few minutes. Does anything come to mind? Any gentle prompting? Write it down!

On Learning to Listen

Okay, since this is the biggest issue in learning to walk with God, let's give this some more attention.

This is Step One in learning to listen to the voice of God: Ask simple questions. You cannot start with huge and desperate questions like, "Should I marry Ted?" "Do you want me to sell the family business tomorrow?" or "Do I have lung cancer?" (Paranoia rarely enables me to hear God's voice.) That's like learning to play the piano by starting with Mozart, learning to ski by doing double black diamonds. There is way too much emotion involved, too much swirling around in our heads. I find that to hear the voice of God, we must be in a posture of quiet surrender. Starting with small questions helps us learn to do that.

A gentle whisper. A still small voice, as some translations have it. To hear that gentle whisper, we have to settle down. Shut out all the drama. Quiet our hearts. Now, as we grow in our personal holiness, we can be quiet and surrendered even in the major questions. But that takes time, and maturity. Don't ask that of yourself as you are starting out. Begin with simple questions. I can sit quietly with the question, *What do you want for this weekend?*

Should we go to the ranch, or stay home? It's not a life and death matter. I am not desperately hoping to hear what I secretly want to hear. There is not a great deal of drama around it.

What I'll do is sit with the question before God for several minutes. To help me stay present to God and not begin to wander (*Did I take the socks out of the dryer? Is tomorrow the phone call with my publisher? Where did I leave my cell phone?*), I will repeat the question quietly in my heart. *God—do you want us to go to the ranch or stay home?* I am settling myself before God. *Do you want us to go to the ranch or stay home?* Settle down, and be present to God. Pause, and listen. Repeat the question. *Should we go to the ranch or stay home? What is your counsel* (pages 26–27)?

Let's do that right now. Jot down here a couple of small, simple questions to ask God. Settle yourself down. Get quiet. And ask one of the questions. Quietly repeat it in your heart. What do you hear?

Clarity

Let me say what I mean by "hear." I don't believe God speaks "out loud" in the same way you would try to get your neighbor's attention over the back fence. I believe he "speaks" in our hearts, inside of us. It's an internal voice.

Now, sometimes as we set out to learn to hear God's voice, what we first can "hear" is more of a "prompting" or a "comfort" giving us an answer to our question. In other words, sometimes what we get is more of an impression than a clearly perceived word or sentence. That's okay. That's good. It's a beginning. That's your answer. And sometimes, when I'm having a hard time perceiving an actual word from God, he'll do something playful like my eye will fall on the page of my open Bible and a passage will "jump off the page" or my eye will fall directly on a word and it fits the question perfectly.

So, be open to hearing an actual word or phrase from God internally, somewhat like you hear your own thoughts. But be open to other ways he might speak, such as an "impression" or by seeing something actually written down that God uses to speak to you.

"But how do I know it's God and not my own thoughts?"

It's a good question. My answer is, "you will over time." As you practice learning to listen to Jesus' voice, you'll know when you are "filling in the blanks" and when he is speaking. But to help you along the way, let me offer this: First, listen to your own thoughts for a bit. Get accustomed to them. While you are sitting quietly, say a few things to yourself inside, internally. *Hello, David. These are your own thoughts speaking to you. Did you pay the water bill? Do you have a yellow duck?* This helps you get used to the sound of your own thoughts, so that you can distinguish them from God speaking.

Next, begin to intentionally quiet your own thoughts. Make an effort to simply shut down all the internal chatter. Be still, as the Scripture says, and know that I am God. Learning to silence your own thoughts will help you make room for God to speak. (I know, I know, sometimes it seems like our thoughts have a life of their own and it's loud in there. Be patient. You will learn to quiet all that with practice.)

Here's another helpful tool to know if that thought that just came to you or that voice you just "heard" inside is from God or not: test the fruit of it. If you embrace the thought as from God, as being true, what is the fruit? Does it bring hope, love, joy, comfort? That sounds like God. Does it bring sorrow or discouragement, or worse, accusation and self-reproach? God is not the accuser; Satan is. So if you hear condemning things you know that's not from God (Romans 8:1).

Here's something else I do quite a bit: ask Jesus to confirm what you think you've just heard him say. For instance, you've just heard a "Go to Cleveland," in answer to your question, "Should we visit my parents this Christmas." (They live in Cleveland). Pause, and ask for confirmation. "Jesus, are you saying go to Cleveland?" He will say something like "Yes," or "Right," or "Go to Cleveland."

Now, if I don't seem to be able to hear his voice in that moment, sometimes what I will do is "try on" one answer, and then the other. Still in a posture of quiet surrender, I will ask the Lord, *Is it Yes, you want us to go?* Pause. In my heart, I am trying it on, letting it be as though this is God's answer. *We should go?* Pause, and listen. *Or is it, No, you want us to stay home?* Pause, and let this be his answer. Try it on. *We should stay home?* Pause, and listen.

Quite often we can sense God's direction on a matter before we hear actual words. You may have heard someone use the expression, "I had a check in my spirit." It refers to an internal pause, a hesitancy, a sudden reluctance to proceed. The Spirit of God may be impressing you with the will of God by making one answer seem very unappealing, or wrong somehow. Arresting you, stopping you. Our spirit is in union with the Spirit of God, and his Spirit is often making his will known to us deep within us, before it forms into words. By "trying on" the possible answers, I find it enables me to come into alignment with his Spirit. And, over time, those deep impressions begin to form into words. A simple yes or no can be so encouraging as we learn to listen.

WHOLE AND HOLY

Now for another core assumption about the Christian life, and especially about learning to walk with God—true holiness requires the healing of our souls.

> How blessed is God! And what a blessing he is! He's the Father of our Master, Jesus Christ, and takes us to the high places of blessing in him. Long before he laid down earth's foundations, he had us in mind, had settled on us as the focus of his love, to be made whole and holy by his love (Ephesians 1: 3–4, *The Message*) (page 30).

Whole and holy. The two go hand in hand. Oh, how important this is. You can't find the holiness you want without deep wholeness. And you can't find the wholeness you want without deep holiness.

What do you make of that? Is this what you've been taught? What do the folks in your church community believe about holiness?

My drivenness and compulsion will ruin me if they continue. God knows that. He also knows what I need. Sitting here on the porch I am asking him to come into the deep places of my soul and heal me. I know, at least in part, what this is rooted in. Early on in my life I found myself alone. It was a deep and profound wounding. No boy is meant to be on his own. But with that wounding came a sinful resolution—*I will make it on my own.* I felt that life was up to me (that was my wounding). I resolved to live as though life was up to me (that was my sin). The path to be free of all this pushing and striving involves *both* repentance and healing (page 32).

What I am describing here is the dynamic between our brokenness and our sin. The two work together against us. And if we would really find true and lasting freedom, real transformation, we have to deal with both. So, I want you to think of a struggle you'd love to be free of. Large or small. Can you see both sin and brokenness involved? Describe that. (And if not, if it's a mystery to you, try asking Jesus, "Lord, what is my sin in this, and what is my need for healing?")

To be made whole and holy by his love. Listen to Jesus,

> For this people's heart has become calloused;
> they hardly hear with their ears,
> and they have closed their eyes.
> Otherwise they might see with their eyes,
> hear with their ears,
> understand with their hearts
> and turn, and I would heal them. (Matthew 13:15)

Heal them. Jesus yearned for his people to turn back to him *so that he could heal them!* This is so essential to your view of the gospel. It will shape your convictions about nearly everything else. God wants to restore us (pages 32–33).

Pause. Do you believe this—that God wants to restore you? I don't mean you think it might be true or it sounds like a nice thought—do you believe that God wants to restore *you?* Why—or why not?

Our part is to "turn," to repent as best we can. But we also need his healing. As Ephesians says, God chose us to make us whole and holy through his love (1:4). God will make known to us the path of life, if we will follow him. And as we do, we find along that path our need for wholeness and holiness.

And so I'm praying, and journaling,

> Jesus, forgive me. I ask your forgiveness of this deep commitment to make life work on my own. For all my striving and pushing and for all the unbelief that propels them. Forgive me.
>
> And I ask you to heal me of this. Heal the places in my soul that have so long felt alone, felt that life was up to me (page 33).

I will often do just this—write out my prayers in my journal. It helps me to focus, and also to come back to it later. Write your own prayer out now, asking Jesus both for forgiveness (that's your part—repent-ing) and asking for healing in this very struggle of yours.

🌿 Pause now and listen. What is God saying to you?

MAKING ROOM FOR JOY

I came to a number of important revelations over the year I wrote the book. This is one of them—that joy is essential, that the battle in our lives is against joy, and that for the most part we don't think about it much. We've all moved into a sort of survival mode.

> For several days the whole world made sense in light of joy. But in the day-to-day grind of the ensuing months, all that clarity slipped away. Completely. Joy as a category seemed . . . irrele-vant. Nice, but unessential. Like owning a hot tub. And distant too. The hot tub is in Fiji. Wouldn't it be nice? Ain't going to happen. Life's not really about Joy. I've got all this *stuff* that has to get done. The mail is stacking up and I haven't paid the bills

in two months. The "fix engine" light came on in the Honda. Joy? Life's about surviving, and getting a little pleasure. That's what seemed true (page 34).

How do you see this mindset operating in your life? What "seems true" about life to you?

Really now—how much do you think about joy? Do you see it as essential to your life, something God insists on?

It has to do with agreements I've made without even knowing it. By "agreement" I mean those subtle convictions we come to, or assent to, or give way to. It happens down deep in our souls where our real beliefs about life are formed. Something or someone whispers to us, *Life is never going to turn out the way you'd hoped*, or, *Nobody's going to come through*, or, *God has forsaken you*. And something in us responds with, *That's true*. We make an agreement with it. A conviction is formed. It seems so reasonable. I think we come to more of our beliefs in this way than maybe any other. Subtle agreements.

Anyhow, I begin to realize that what I've done for most of my life is resign myself to this idea: *I'm really not going to have any lasting joy.* And from that resignation I have gone on to try and find what I could have. Women do this in marriage. They see there is not going to be any real intimacy with their husband, so they lose themselves in soaps or tabloids or romance novels. Men find their work a sort of slow death, so they get a little something in the bar scene each night. Have a few beers with the boys, watch the game. Joy isn't even a consideration. Settle for relief (pages 35–36).

⚜ Can you relate to this? Might you have made a similar agreement about joy? Can you name it?

⚜ Where do you turn for a little comfort, a little relief?

⚜ What *do* you believe about joy?

I am going to talk more about agreements throughout the book, but let me pause here to underscore how very important they are in defining our lives, our view of God and ourselves, our *interpretation* of events. Agreements shape us very deeply. And here is where listening to God can bring some real relief. Most of the awareness I have about agreements I've made has come through asking Jesus to reveal them. So I want you to pause, and ask Jesus,

Lord, teach me about agreements. Show me what agreements I've made. I ask you to reveal them. Especially here and now, about joy. What do I believe about joy, Lord?

Write down anything you hear, or think of or suddenly now remember.

But joy *is* the point. I know it is. God says that joy is our strength: "The joy of the LORD is your strength" (Nehemiah 8:10). "My heart leaps with joy" (Psalm 28:7). "You have filled my heart with greater joy than when their grain and new wine abound" (Psalm 4:7).

"I have told you this so that my joy may be in you and that your joy may be complete" (John 15:11). "Until now you have not asked for anything in my name. Ask and you will receive, and your joy will be complete" (John 16:24). "I am coming to you now, but I say these things while I am still in the world, so that they may have the full measure of my joy within them" (John 17:13).

⫷ What is happening in your heart as you read these passages on joy?

I wrote that, "Joy is such a tender thing, I think we resent it. We avoid it, because it feels too vulnerable to allow ourselves to admit the joy we long for but do not have." And then I simply wrote a short prayer to Jesus: "*Jesus, I have no idea where to go from here. But I invite you in. Take me where I need to go. I know this is connected to the life you want me to live* (see page 37)."

⫷ Write out a prayer of your own now, talking to the Lord about joy and what this entry has stirred in you.

WHAT SHOULD I READ?

We need God to help us understand his Word. We can't separate a walk with God from your reading of Scripture. The two go hand-in-hand. Like having a tour guide as you wander the halls of the Louvre. "If you love me, you will obey what I command. And I will ask the Father, and he will give you another Counselor to be with you forever—the Spirit of truth. The world cannot accept him, because it neither sees him nor knows him. But you know him, for he lives with you and will be in you" (John 14:15–17). Too many people approach the Scripture without an intimacy with God, and they either end up frustrated because they've gotten so little out of it, or, far worse, they amass an intellectual understanding quite apart from any real communion with God. It usually results in religious pride. The Bible was meant to be read in fellowship with God. Things get really weird if we don't (page 38).

🌾 Can you see this in the folks you know, maybe the people in your own church?

🌾 Can you see it in your own life?

Now, I'm all for the various programs available to help you read through the Bible in a year, or study a certain book. It helps so much to know context, and history. We have the benefit of commentaries, and concordances, all sorts of electronic Bible study software—I use them all and benefit from them. But in addition to all that, let me add how rich it can be simply to ask God, *What would you have me read today?*

Letting your Shepherd lead you in your reading allows him to take you right to a passage that you might not have thought of yourself, might not have been in line with the recent program you were using, but is the *very* word you need. In this way I have received so many warnings, immeasurable counsel, comfort beyond number, and simply the incomparable intimacy of God speaking directly to me through his Word (page 40).

⚜ Does this sound attractive to you? Available to you personally?

⚜ Have you ever tried this—asked God what to read?

Clarity

I told the story of hearing God tell me one morning to read John. As I turned to the gospel of John, I kept asking "Where, Lord?" And after a few moments I heard Ten. This sort of "tuning into God" takes time, and practice. Sometimes, I don't hear anything. In those cases I simply read what seems good to read. But I don't want to get discouraged because sometimes I'm not hearing anything from God. Because there have been thousands of times I have heard. So stick with it.

Now, I'm usually praying and reading first thing in the morning. I find that FIRST, I usually have to pray through what I call my "Daily Prayer" because I need to realign myself with God, sanctify my life, and shut down the warfare the enemy is bringing against me. Those three things are crucial.

Realign yourself with God. We are barraged every day with thousands of messages from all sorts of media—billboards, television, magazines, email, the Internet, etc. It is overwhelmingly *distracting*. It pulls our focus away from God. And we get busy, running like mad, and we wander away from God ourselves. So, we need to realign with God every day. Come back under his Lordship. Bring our thoughts captive to Christ. Trying to listen without doing this is like trying to hold a conversation with a friend while you are driving eighty on the interstate in heavy traffic while listening to rock music blasting on the stereo.

Sanctify your life. This, too, is crucial. We present ourselves again to God.

Don't even begin to draw conclusions about whether or not you can hear from God until you've practiced these three things. In fact, do it now. Pray through the Daily Prayer, at the back of this guide.

Give it a try. Ask God what he would have you read. Settle yourself, quiet your heart. Take all the pressure off that you *have* to hear from him right now or things aren't well between you. Things are fine. You are his. Rest your heart and your relationship there. Then ask this simple question, *God, what would you have me read today?* Pause, and listen. Repeat the question. If you begin to get an impression, or believe you heard him say something, repeat it. *Was that John ten Lord? You want me to read John ten?* (That "trying it on" thing.) Practice this over the course of several weeks.

Begin now. Ask God what he would have you read.

WHEN WE DON'T HEAR GOD

The story I told about looking for my watch—was that helpful?

Let me highlight two very important points. First, "We don't know on any given day all that's playing into why we can't seem to hear from God."

> It could be I'm still too distracted, obsessed with finding it myself. It could be the enemy is blocking me. It could be God isn't going to speak on this right now . . . But I do know this—it can't be the verdict of how I'm doing with God or how he feels about me in this moment.
>
> Hearing from God *flows out of* our relationship. That relationship was established for us by Jesus Christ. "Therefore, since we have been justified [made right with God] through faith, have peace with God through our Lord Jesus Christ, through whom

we have gained access by faith into this grace in which we now stand" (Romans 5:1–2). Whatever we might be feeling, we do have relationship with God now, because we belong to him. And our relationship is secure. "For I am convinced that neither death nor life, neither angels nor demons, neither the present nor the future, nor any powers, neither height nor depth, nor anything else in all creation, will be able to separate us from the love of God that is in Christ Jesus our Lord" (Romans 8:38–39). I am God's. He is mine (page 45).

My ability to hear his voice on any given day does not change that one bit.

Second, if you are having a hard time hearing from God on a particular question, "Keep praying. Keep listening. Notice what God might be up to other than answering the immediate question." This is HUGE. It may be that God wants to speak to you about something else! And so, what you can do is ask God, *Is there something else you want to say to me today?* Sometimes he just wants to say, *I love you.*

And ask God, *Is there a different question you want to answer? What question should I be asking?* You might find that this opens up the conversation for you.

An hour and a half has gone by, now it's time for me to leave, and I really would love to have my watch. So I pray again, *Jesus, help me find my watch.* I'm not pushing into hearing right now, I'm trusting something deeper—that he's here, and that he can guide me in other ways. This isn't an all-or-nothing proposition. It's not either I hear from God or he isn't involved. Not at all. I go into the bedroom, grab a pair of socks out of the drawer, and sit down in the middle of the floor to put them on. I don't think I've ever done that before, sat down in this particular spot to put on my socks. But from this angle I can see under the bed. And there it is. My watch (page 47).

Let your heart rest in this—God can speak to you through all sorts of means. I'll pray about something, and the next Sunday it's the very thing the pastor is preaching on. Or a friend will offer some words to me, and it's the very thing I needed to hear. Or—this has happened to me many times—I'll be driving down the road and there's a billboard with the very words of my answer in large letters. God is creative. He speaks in many ways.

How has he been speaking to you?

YOU SHALL KNOW THEM BY THEIR FRUITS

The first major awakening in our journey of faith is coming to realize that God exists. It can be quite a jolt. The second, and far more life-changing epiphany, is when we come to realize that we have to deal with him. Take him into account. We come to see that God is not to be ignored. This is an even bigger jolt, and a major course correction for any human being. Many people avoid it for years. But hopefully, we come to see that there is no better way than to place our love and trust in God, accept his invitation to life, and give our hearts to him. We become his sons and daughters through faith in Jesus Christ. And hopefully, his followers.

But there is another major awakening. The next epiphany in our journey of faith is coming to realize that Satan exists. And that we have to deal with him, too. Take him into account. We come to realize that he is not to be ignored, either. I'm sorry to say that this awakening is uncommon, even among the followers of Christ. Despite the fact that the Scripture is filled with warnings of an enemy (page 49).

❧ Okay, be honest—have you come to this major awakening that you have an enemy? Do you factor that into the way you evaluate daily events?

Let's come back to the naïve assumption that A + B = C. Be good. Believe in God. And all will be well. *No*, Jesus said. *There is more going on here. You have an enemy. You've got to take that into account, or you won't find the life I am offering you.*

Let that sink in—you won't find the life God is offering you until you deal with the enemy. What life are you longing for that hasn't come to you? Have you considered that Satan might be involved? Have you prayed against him?

You shall know them, Jesus said, by their fruits.

The principle holds true for anything in life. It is especially helpful in diagnosing what the enemy might be up to. What is the fruit of what you're experiencing? What is its *effect*? If it continues, what will the results of that be? What will be lost?

This is SUCH a helpful tool—judging things by their fruit. What's not going well in your life these days? What will be the fruit if it continues not to go well?

So, who might be involved, based on that fruit?

Do It Now

I have to pray about this *now*.

But whenever I'm facing spiritual attack of any kind, the pull is *nearly always* to try and ignore it, or push it off till later, or explain it away as bad digestion or my ongoing inadequacies or something else. Anything else. I see this in all my friends as well. We just don't want to deal with it.

God gave us a will. Learning to exercise it is a great part of maturing as a person. You don't want to get out of bed in the morning? You'll lose your job. You don't want to deny yourself anything? You'll go into debt. This is Growing Up 101. And there is no place like spiritual warfare to teach you to exercise your will. For one thing, you won't want to deal with it. So the best thing you can do is turn, face the attack, and deal with it.

Now. It strengthens your will. But then what most Christians do is they end up not really praying against it directly. They'll pray something like, "Jesus, I ask you to take this away." If it's discouragement they're dealing with, they'll pray something like, "I ask you to encourage me." And it's a good thing to be encouraged. Or let's say it's lust you've been confronted with. Most folks will then pray, "Give me pure thoughts, Lord." And it's a good thing to ask for pure thoughts.

But you're still dodging the issue (pages 50–51).

Can you relate? Do you see this kind of dodging in your own life? Where?

The enemy is present, in the form of some foul spirit, and *you* must command him to leave. As the Scripture urges, "Resist the devil and he will flee from you" (James 4:7). No resist, no flee. We are *commanded* to resist. "Finally Paul became so troubled that he turned around and said to the spirit, 'In the name of Jesus Christ I command you to come out of her!' At that moment the spirit left her" (Acts 16:18). Out loud. In the name of Jesus Christ. That's how it's done. Now, it really helps if you can name the spirit. You are dealing with a distorted being here, a foul spirit filled with disobedience and deception. They will duck and maneuver and refuse to leave. You've got to be direct, and you've got to be authoritative. "'Be quiet!' Jesus said sternly" (Luke 4:35). Note the "sternly."

Sometimes you know what you are dealing with by its fruit. You're suddenly slammed with lust—then it's Lust you must banish. You're under a malaise of despair—then it's Despair you must banish. But even better at this point is to *stop and ask God* what you're dealing with. Don't just swing wildly away at it. Ask Jesus what you need to pray against. As you grow in your ability to hear his voice, this will become *so* very helpful in dealing with the enemy (page 51).

So, what's been harassing you lately? Can you name it? Discouragement? Unbelief? Anger? Stop, and name it right now. And, ask Jesus what is set against you today.

So here is how I prayed this morning: "I bring the kingdom of God and the glory of the Lord Jesus Christ, I bring the fullness of the work of Christ against this spirit of distraction, and against all foul spirits here." Distraction doesn't quite seem to hit the mark, so I ask God, *What is it, Lord—what am I dealing with here? Diminishment,* he says. Oh yes, that's been an enemy of mine for many years. Okay. "I bring the full work of the Lord Jesus Christ against Diminishment, and I bind Diminishment from me." Remember, Jesus says "bind the strong man" (Matthew 12:29) (page 52).

Now it's your turn. Pray like this against the enemies you've just named. Do it now. (And remember, sometimes it takes a few whacks to get these guys to obey. It's like felling a tree—one pass often doesn't quite get the job done. The more you practice this, the more comfortable you'll get with it.) Pray like this:

"I bring the kingdom of God and the glory of the Lord Jesus Christ, I bring the fullness of the work of Jesus Christ against (name what it is that has been harassing you). I bring the full work of the Lord Jesus Christ against (name it again) and I bind all this from me in the Name of my Lord Jesus Christ."

Clarity

You should start noticing a difference. Feeling better. Sometimes these things take a bit of time to be worked out in the spiritual realm. So if you don't experience relief in the next thirty minutes or so, stop and pray like this again. Quite often Satan will test our resolve, just as he did with Christ in the wilderness. Once he sees that we mean business, then you will experience the joy of the second half of James 4:7, " . . . and he will flee from you."

BEWARE OF AGREEMENTS

Let's focus a bit more on agreements. As I mentioned before, agreements are often quite subtle, but oh, so powerful in their negative effect upon our lives. What is your response to the story about Anne?

I told this story in part because of the correlation to hearing from God, or, in this case, not being able to hear from God. Take note! If you are feeling discouraged in your efforts to hear God's voice, well—look at the fruit of that. Who would love to discourage you? Who would love for you to decide, *This is just not for me*? Satan, of course. SO, you may find that on certain days you will need to pray against the enemy in order to open up the channels to hear from God. Let this be a category or evaluation for you. Remember Anne's story!

But Anne's story is about so much more than spiritual warfare. It is an example of how agreements "get in" when we are vulnerable or distressed or just terribly disappointed. We all make them, by the way. The question is not "Have I made an agreement" but rather "What are they? When did they get in?" It might be a very good idea to pause right now, and ask Jesus, *Lord, what agreements have I made? What is pinning my heart down? Come and reveal the agreements I've made even now.*

Listen. Write down what comes to mind.

Now you must break them!!! This is how:

Lord Jesus, thank you for revealing these agreements. Forgive me for making them. I renounce the lies of my enemy. Here and now I break the agreement I've made with (fill in the blank—what are they?). I renounce these lies, and I renounce every claim I've given to these lies in my life. Come to me here, in these very places, Lord Jesus. Heal my heart here. Remind me of what is true. In your name I pray.

BEING WILLING TO HAVE A LOOK

Next we move to the story of my old Land Cruiser, how I didn't want to face the fact that I may have let my oil run down and may have ruined my engine.

When was the last time I checked the oil? I can't remember that, either. A sort of discomfort-becoming-dread fills my stomach, like ice water. It's one thing to forget to keep your radiator filled. If things go wrong, you'll typically find out right away because your car overheats and steam comes blowing out. But by the time you realize you blew it with your oil, deeper damage has usually been done to your engine. Like a faithful old camel, this Land Cruiser will run till it drops. But you don't want to do that to a car. You don't want to find out you forgot to add oil by having your engine seize. Now, I'm standing there knowing all this, knowing I need to check the oil *now* . . . but something in me hesitates.

I don't want to know.

I don't want to go there.

I know it's been a long time. And I don't know that I really want the information that lies at the end of my dipstick (pages 58–59).

Sound familiar? Anything like this going on in your life? What are you avoiding these days?

What have you been avoiding for years?

We do this with our internal life most of all. Something will come up to cause us to realize it's been a long time (have we ever, really?) since we had a look under the hood. An argument with our spouse. A sudden and very strong pull to someone else's spouse. Fear over a coming presentation. Anxiety. Depression. Someone else simply asking the question, "How are you doing?" We sense rumblings beneath the surface, and we don't want to go there (page 59).

Any "rumblings" causing you to be uneasy lately? Emotions from out of nowhere? Desires that seem too strong to resist? Maybe just the discomfort you are now feeling as I probe a little here? Name it.

Dear friends, this may be one of the essential differences between those who experience God and the life he offers, and those who don't. Be willing to take a look. I wrote out a simple prayer to Jesus:

Lord Jesus, I want to shift my posture in this. I want to stop avoiding disruption. I want to be willing to have a look under the hood, whenever and wherever you are prompting me. I want to cultivate a willingness to go wherever it is I need to go to face my life. Especially when it comes to the internal issues. I love my old Land Cruiser, but it's a pretty small thing when compared with my heart, and my walk with you. I give my yes to you now (page 61).

≋ Now write yours. What have you been avoiding? Where do you need his help, including the help to be willing to face it?

Now Is the Time

God gives to us dozens of these encounters every day, these opportunities to be honest about what motivates us. What we do with them is up to us.

Whatever else we do with these moments, let us be honest about one thing—there is no getting to it later. We don't get to it later. It simply goes away. And I wonder—how often do we say to ourselves, "I'll get to it later" *knowing* that it never happens, and thus we appease our conscience in the moment *and* avoid the issue, let it slip away under the ruse of "later."

So—how do we walk with God in the day to day, in the moment? We go with it. Now. As it is unfolding. That is the only way to have any real relationship with Jesus Christ.

We've been working through a lot of really core issues already in this guide—how to listen to God, judging things by their fruit, joy, how to resist the enemy, the power of agreements, the disruptions that cause us to take a deeper look at our lives. But where all this gets lived out is not so much in these exercises, but in the moment to moment living of our lives.

Rest

It's so quiet. And I absolutely love it. No email. No phone to answer. My cell phone doesn't get reception here. Everyone I know is at least four hours away. Maybe I'll make a peanut butter and jelly sandwich for dinner because I don't want to make dinner. And the best part of the peace and quiet is God. Just to sit here and be with God. No agenda. Nothing to be fought for or prayed over. Just God. It's like nothing else. Nothing even comes close. This is what the moment offers now. This is what God is up to today. And thankfully, I am going with it now, by resting with him (page 63).

Where can you find some rest this week? How will you make sure you take those opportunities?

WHAT GOD *IS* GIVING

In this entry I told three stories of wanting one thing, and God giving another—the Bear River, the hawk, and the sunset on the Snake River canoe trip.

Then I remembered something God has been teaching me this summer—it's not what he isn't giving, but what he *is* giving. We can get so locked onto what we don't have, what we think we want or need, that we miss the gifts God is giving. Really, though the river had proved to be everything I hoped the creek would be—solitude, beauty, wild fish on a dry fly—I sulked half way back to the car because I didn't get my creek (page 65).

🌾 What disappointments have been dominating the landscape of your life lately?

🌾 Now, those disappointments may be very real. But in spite of those, what *has* God been bringing into your life, what gifts has he been giving? It might help you to name them here.

ON ELK AND ELIJAH

Before we dive into the lessons of this story, allow me to state the obvious: You don't have to be a hunter to glean from stories like this one the deeper truths, the gifts God is giving. You don't have to drive an old truck, or be a writer, or a father, or have a friend named Anne. While the DETAILS of my stories are particular to my life, the lessons are UNIVERSAL. Just thought it would be good to point that out. Because a very subtle agreement the enemy could try to bring in is, "Well, that's just John's deal. This doesn't really apply."

And, may I also point out that there are SO many lessons-within-the-lesson of each story. One of the Big Ones here is about prayer.

One of my favorite Old Testament stories is the one about Elijah praying for rain.

> Elijah climbed to the top of Carmel, bent down to the ground and put his face between his knees. "Go and look toward the sea," he told his servant. And he went up and looked. "There is nothing there," he said. Seven times Elijah said, "Go back." The seventh time the servant reported, "A cloud as small as a man's hand is rising from the sea." So Elijah said, "Go and tell Ahab, 'Hitch up your chariot and go down before the rain stops you.'" Meanwhile, the sky grew black with clouds, the wind rose, a heavy rain came on . . . (1 Kings 18:42–45).

I love it that he kept sending his servant to have a look. Is it working? I love it that it took this mighty man seven rounds of prayer to get it going. This story is so true to life. And now for the really wild thought—James says we can do it too. Towards the end of his epistle, James is trying to encourage us to pray like we mean it. After the famous passage, "The prayer of a righteous man is powerful and effective," James points to this story as the example: "Elijah was a man just like us. He prayed earnestly that it would not rain, and it did not rain on the land for three and a half years. Again he prayed, and the heavens gave rain, and the earth produced its crops" (5:17–18).

Now—why does he make the point of saying that Elijah "was a man just like us"?

Because of that thing in each of us that says, *I could never do that*. Because of that theology that says, "Those stories are exceptions." That sort of thinking cripples faith. It cuts your prayer life off at the knees. Why are we given stories about the power of godly people praying if our prayers really don't accomplish anything? No, James says, he was just like you and me. This is no exception. Meaning, you can do this too. You can pray and see things happen.

Now remember—how many times did Elijah have to take a whack at it? Did it come on the first round? The second? The third?

Too many times our prayers are wimpy little prayers like, "Jesus, be with us." He is with you. Always. Or we pray, "Lord, give us good weather today." And that's it. One round, and we quit. And then we are discouraged when our prayers don't seem to do anything, and we come to the conclusion that prayer really doesn't work. It would be more accurate to say prayers like *that* don't work. Start praying like Elijah and maybe you'll see some results (pages 68–70).

How would you describe your prayer life? Let's say a close friend, someone you feel fine confiding in, just asked you, "So tell me about your prayers? How do you pray? How often? What's it sound like?" What would you say?

Let's take this a step at a time. James says Elijah was a person just like you. The reason he includes that is because so many of us think,

I could never do that. Right? Have you felt that way, reading Bible stories?

🖐 And he says there is really no difference between you and Elijah because of that theology that goes, "Those stories are exceptions." Have you bought into that thinking?

That sort of thinking really does cripple faith. It cuts your prayer life off right at the knees. Why would God give you stories about the power of godly people praying if your prayers really can't accomplish much? These are *examples*!!! You can do this too. You can pray and see things happen. But remember—how many times did Elijah have to pray in order to get the rain coming? Once? Twice? How many times?

I want you to take a swing at this—learning to pray with much more intention and determination, in a manner similar to Elijah. Pick something you really want to see some change in. (Or better, far better, ask Jesus what he'd have you pray about!). Go at it for several days, not just once but seven times, every time you pray.

"MY LOVE"

I described in this entry a habit I've gotten into which has become very dear to me. Often as I am going through my day I'll turn my heart and thoughts toward God simply to ask him, *What are you saying, Lord?* It's my way of checking in with God. I'll do it as I drive, or as I sit at my desk, I'll do it while I'm watching my kids play sports, whenever.

I want you to give it a try. Begin to simply turn your thoughts and heart towards God as you move through your day. Listen for his voice. Lord, what are you saying to me?

Now, I confessed that sometimes God will say something that doesn't seem to "fit" the situation. I might be asking for guidance, and all he wants me to hear at that moment is how much he loves me. So, be open to this, to God saying something other than what you think you need to hear.

Now, to the love of God. Throughout the entire year of writing this book, the one thing God spoke to me about more than any other was some reminder of his love. I don't think I'm the only one who needs these reminders. Let me ask you—how often do you feel loved by God, I mean, as a experiential reality?

Maybe it would be good for you to pray, "Lord Jesus, open my eyes to see the way you are showing me your love. Open my ears to hear your words of love to me." And then, keep an eye out and an ear open for his replies.

Fall

A Season of Crisis and Struggle, but then Breakthrough and Discovery

THE ACCIDENT

What was your initial response to this story? What did it stir in you?

Clarify

Now, I mentioned earlier that there are lessons within the lesson of each of these little entries. I made an aside in this story that I want to highlight here:

> That's a really important part of listening to God, by the way. Ask the *next* question. I think so often we get an answer to the first part of a question, but fail to ask the second half. We hear a, *Yes, take the job*. Or, *Yes, sell the house*. But then we need to ask, *When? Today, next week, next year?* Don't just get a first impression and then blast ahead. It might have been good for us to ask, *Where should we ride (Walking with God*, page 77)*?*

Ask the next question! Don't just get what you think is an answer or a green light. Stay with the conversation a little longer, ask the Lord for more. Let's say you've been asking God if you should have that difficult conversation with your mother or a friend. If you sense a yes, or a no, ask him to say more. "When should I bring this up, Lord?" "How should I bring this up?"

I can't say strongly enough how important this is. Sometimes in the joy and excitement of learning to hear from God, we get an answer and we just rush off without getting further counsel on the matter.

Okay, now we enter into some deeper waters, now we begin to tackle the hard things in life. Our pain and suffering.

> But it's a little late for that now. And you can really chase your tail on this sort of thing and get nothing but all tied up in knots. When it comes to crises or events that really upset us, this I have learned—you can have God, or you can have understanding. Sometimes you can have both. But if you *insist* on understanding, it often doesn't come. And that can create distance between you and God, because you're upset and demanding an explanation in order to move on, but the explanation isn't coming, and so you withdraw a bit from God. And lose the grace that God *is* giving. He doesn't explain everything. But he always offers us himself (page 77).

This is HUGE. I find it very hard to hear from God when I am in deep distress or anguish, especially if all I am asking is for an explanation. Can you relate? What have you hoped that God would explain to you that you haven't been able to understand?

In the deepest moments of pain in my life, I have learned this time and again: you can have God, or you can have understanding. I'm not sure of all of the reasons for this. But let me ask you—are you willing to settle for God, and let go of your insistence on understanding?

It might be helpful to return to an event in your life, some loss or pain where you felt you "lost" God somewhat because he wasn't speaking and you were in distress, and maybe what was happening was that you were waiting for an explanation and it didn't come so you walked away. Invite God back into that time and event, that particular issue. Let go of the need to understand. Ask God to be near. Let him be enough.

I explained that right after the accident, even as we left the hospital, what I was watching for was not God's explanation of why I got hurt, but rather, what comes next. What would I do with what happened? What would God do with it?

Right now, what I'm aware of is how shaken I am by what happened. I'm realizing that my life is going to be radically changed for some time. I'm heartbroken as I start realizing the losses that come with this. I've lost archery season, all that time with Blaine and the guys. I can't tie my shoes, let alone pull a bow. Sam and I have been building a car together, and now that's lost for who knows how long. It's his first car, and we were rebuilding it together. I won't be able to help. I know I *really* want God to heal me. And I'm very aware of how much I don't want to be in a place of need.

My whole approach to life has been built on be tough, need nothing, push through. I hated wearing that little hospital gown, the one that doesn't really tie in back. I insisted that Stasi put my boots on when it was time to leave. As we drove home from the emergency room in Steamboat Springs, my cell phone began to ring. Stasi had called a friend on the way to the hospital to ask for prayer. Word got out, and friends began checking in. I was so completely blown away by the amount of love and concern. And I noticed something.

I have a *real* hard time being loved.

It's hard to accept a fundamental reorientation of your approach to life. The old ways are so deeply woven into our personalities, so grounded in our core assumptions, so rooted in our wounds, and in what has worked for us over the years. And there is nothing like a crisis to expose all of it. So long as our old ways are working, we really aren't open to looking at them. Let alone giving them up. But then something like this happens. Now I'm backed into a corner. This disruption is going to be far more than physical. Whatever else may come out of this, I want to be transformed. I mean, love is pretty central to life after all. I don't think it's a good idea to miss out on love (pages 78–79).

If there was a soundtrack that accompanied this book, right now what you would be hearing would be one of the climactic moments in the score. This is one of the BIG issues—accepting a fundamental reorientation of our approach to life. Let me see if I can help you connect this to your own story. What has been really hard for you this year? It might be an injury, it might be more of an emotional suffering, it might not be dramatic, but what has been really hard for you this year?

And how does this trial, this suffering or pain disrupt you? I talked about how I attack life, and how I hate being in a place of need. How my accident put me in a profound place of need, and that was *so* disrupting. How has you pain been disrupting to you?

I can't drive. I can't open a door. Opening a bottle of juice is impossible. So is cutting a steak. Oh, man. I am going to need help with *everything*. I can't even button a button. Whatever else might be going on here, this accident is thwarting my entire approach to life. I see it now. My approach to life is so fundamentally based upon Charge or Attack. That's how I live. I attack life. I get up in the morning and attack the day. Whatever needs to get done, whatever worries I may have, whatever fears lie underneath, I attack.

But that is not the life I want to live.

And so I come back to your love. You said, My love. I want a life that is based on your love. Rooted and grounded in your love.

It's hard to say clearly enough or with enough force just how important this revelation is. Words like paradigm shift or epiphany just don't quite touch it. As we drove back down the highway from the hospital, me stretched out in the back of the

Suburban, I prayed, *God, I give you permission to rebuild my personality based upon your love* (page 79).

⁂ Can you name, as a sort of confession, what *your* "fundamental approach to life" is? (And if you can't name it, would you be willing to ask God to reveal it to you? And then ask a friend who knows you well to help you name it?)

⁂ Is that the life you want to live? Would you be willing to pray a prayer like I prayed, give God permission to change your personality, even to be built upon his love?

Jesus, I ask you to reveal to me what my fundamental approach to life is. Show me where it got started, back in my story. Show me how deeply I rely on it. And Jesus, I also give you permission to rebuild my personality and my whole approach to life based upon your love.

GOD?

I confessed how I wrestled with God, and why he didn't heal me, heal my wrists. I really struggled with that, especially when so many dear friends were praying for me. What have you struggled with God not doing, or seeming not to come through for you?

> And all the while, in the midst of struggle, I know I have to be careful. This is the vulnerable moment. This is when agreements seem so reasonable, so inescapable.
>
> We have got to be careful with our hearts in this very moment, when we are struggling deeply. I know I cannot give my heart over to anything. "Above all else, guard your heart, for it is the wellspring of life within you" (Proverbs 4:23). The spirit of the passage is this—you've got to be really careful what you give your heart over to. And what you let in your heart. In the midst of this struggle, I know I cannot make agreements with anything. Not discouragement. Not unbelief. Not striving. Not resignation.
>
> It would be so easy to make a subtle agreement down inside, like *Why bother? Prayer doesn't really do anything.* I don't want to go there. I don't know what all God is doing or why it seems at times that our prayers are impotent, but I know this—the only safe place for my heart is in God. Understanding or not, that is where I have to land. I've been through enough hard things to know that eventually there is light on the other side. In the meantime, I know we can shepherd our hearts. We have to (pages 80–81).

No agreements.

Can you see how vulnerable your heart is when you are struggling? Can you name the agreements you may have been making, or made, during that time of struggle.

It might be good to break those agreements now.

Lord Jesus, forgive me for making this agreement with (name it). Forgive me for giving this a hold in my heart. I renounce it now. I reject it, utterly. I banish its hold from my heart and my life. I ask you to come and minister to me here. I invite your Spirit and your love to take the place of this agreement. Lead me in healing. Lead me in the truth. In your name I pray.

Until You Become Our All

"How do we best understand life?" "God wants us to be happy," I said, "But he knows that we cannot be truly happy until we are completely his, and until he is our all. And the weaning process is hard. The sorrows of our lives are in great part his weaning process. We give our hearts over to so many things other than God. We look to so many other things for life. I know I do. Especially the very gifts that he himself gives to us—they become more important to us than he is. It's not the way it was supposed to be. So long as our happiness is tied to the things that we can lose, we are vulnerable."

This truth is core to the human condition and to understanding what God is doing in our lives. We really believe that God is there to provide for our happiness, meaning, to provide us with a good life. As if our fathers are there to provide us with gifts. It doesn't occur to us that we have life backwards. It doesn't even occur to us that God is meant to be our all, and that until he is our all we are subhuman. The first and greatest command is to love God with our whole being. And yet, it's rare to find someone who is completely given over to God. And so normal to be surrounded by people who are trying to make life work. We think of the few who are abandoned to God as sort of odd. The rest of the world (the ones trying to make life work) seems perfectly normal to us (pages 81–82).

Who are the people who have the life you wish you were living? Be honest, now. Don't give the "right" answer or the "spiritual" answer. Who is the living the life you wish you were, or maybe has some aspect of life you wish you had? What is it?

I am really disappointed that life is suddenly beyond my grasp. Literally. The next several months have gone bleak. But do I ever feel this disappointed when God seems distant, when I seem to be losing my grasp of *him*? What is it with us? I am just stunned by this propensity I see in me—and in everyone I know—this stubborn inclination to view the world in one and only one way. As the chance to live a happy little life.

Now, don't get me wrong. There is so much good and beautiful about the world, even though it is fallen. And there is so much good in the life that God gives us. As Paul says, he has given us all things richly to enjoy (1 Timothy 6:17). In Ecclesiastes, Solomon says that to enjoy your work and your food each day is a gift from God (Ecclesiastes 2:24). We are created to enjoy life. But we end up worshiping the gift, not the Giver. We seek for life and look to God as our assistant in the endeavor. We're far more upset when things go wrong than we ever are when we aren't close to God . . . Don't you hear people say, "Why did God let this happen?" far more than you hear them say, "Why aren't I more fully given over to God (pages 82–83)?"

Isn't it true? Can you see this in your friends? In you? What do folks really get upset over?

We see God as a means to an end, rather than the end itself. God as the assistant to our life versus God *as* our life. We don't see the process of our life as coming to the place where we are fully his and he is our all. And so we are surprised by the course of events (page 83).

I hate this, but it's true. So often I see God as a means to an end rather than the greatest goal of my life, my reason for living. Can you relate? How does this manifest itself in your life?

And so God must, from time to time, and sometimes very insistently, disrupt our lives *so that* we release our grasping of life here and now. Usually through pain. God is asking us to let go of the things we love and have given our hearts to, so that we can give our hearts even more fully to him. He thwarts us in our attempts to make life work, so that our efforts fail, and we must face the fact that we don't really look to God for life . . . We are so committed to arranging for a happy little life God has to thwart us to bring us back to himself. It's a kind of regular purging, I suppose. A sort of cleansing for the soul. I have to yield not only all my hopes for this fall, but my basic approach to life as well. Of all tests, I do not want to fail this one (pages 83–84).

What might God be asking you to yield, or to let go of?

And how might he be asking you to give your heart more fully to him?

Now, I am *not* suggesting that God causes all the pain in our lives. I don't believe he pushed me off my horse to make a point. In fact, I believe he saved my life. But pain does come, and what will we do with it? What does it reveal? What might God be up to? How might he redeem it? Those are questions worth asking (page 84).

As my friend Dan says, don't waste your pain.

This approach I am suggesting, to use our pain and disappointments to draw us closer to God—is this the way you've been handling your hardships? Can you see now there might be a better way than simply to make agreements, or get mad at God?

Making Room for God

I told the story of how after the accident I felt God wanted me to quit drinking. (That's continued into the second year, by the way. I have a glass of wine on Thanksgiving or for some celebration, but that's all now). The reason, as I explained, was that I noticed I was drinking too often or drinking for the wrong *reasons.* I'd come home exhausted and frazzled from the day, and I'd turn to a glass of wine or a beer as a sort of refuge and relief, a way to find some peace. Some people use food. Or television.

What do you use? Where do you turn for comfort, or relief, or a taste of joy?

For me, it was alcohol. And God gave me a kind of grace to give it up. To make room in my life for him. What I notice is a kind of spaciousness now in my soul in the evening. Room for God.

Would you be willing to let go of your comforters, to make a little more room in your life for God? Now—before you just jump in, ask Jesus about it.

> "Lord, what would you have me give up for a season, in order to make room in my life for you?"

Stay with that question over the next few days, until you sense his answer.

A Sanctified Life

🌿 What was your initial response to this entry? What did it stir in you?

There's something we need to be honest about. Part of us doesn't really *want* to hear what God has to say. As my friend admitted, "I don't want to ask God if we're supposed to go to Hawaii this year. I just want to go." And I confessed that even after *years* of rescues and surprises and blessing upon blessing, there's a part of me that gets irritated when someone says, "Let's ask God."

🌿 Sound familiar? Are you asking God about most things these days? What are the things you are avoiding asking him about?

If Jesus must tell us to remain in him, then he seems to be assuming that it's quite possible *not* to remain in him. In fact, the common life is a life lived separate from him. And that is a dangerous place to live. We cannot enjoy the fellowship of God, nor his protection, nor all the benefits of his kingdom, unless we remain in him, live in him, in our day-to-day lives. Vine and branches, sheep and shepherd. Stay close. Stay with me.

I want two things that are mutually opposed—I want to live a nice little life, and I want to play an important role in God's kingdom. And it's in those times that I am trying to live a nice little life that I make decisions and choices that cause me in small and subtle ways to simply live outside of Jesus. The shepherd is headed one direction, and I am headed another. Not to some flagrant sin, that's too easy to recognize. I'm simply wandering off looking for the pasture I deem best. I don't even think to ask God about it (pages 85–86).

Sound familiar? How is this playing out in your life right now?

We don't get a normal life, and I think coming to accept that fact and learning to accept it in all the details of our lives is what allows us to remain in Jesus.

This "nice little life" thing is really in the way.

More than anything else, this is what causes me to just wander off on my own, looking for greener pastures. I'm thinking now about how Jesus said, I don't do anything except what the father tells me to do. This is what we are after. It requires a desire to live in God. And it requires a subjected will, and this is where we are made holy. I am not describing the abandonment of our desires, that posture of the soul that says (with resignation), "Just tell me what you want me to do and I'll do it." That's the easy way out. What I am describing is a heart that is present and engaged with God, bringing our desires to him, and yet submitting our will to his, genuinely trusting that what he says is best.

That is how we come to learn to remain in him (pages 87–88).

It might therefore be good to pray,

Jesus, where am I not living close to you, remaining in you these days? What part of my life is not submitted to you? Is there something you are wanting me to surrender?"

Write down what you hear, or what you sense he might be pointing to, or what you simply know isn't submitted to Jesus.

And then ask yourself, *"Why not? Why haven't I been willing to surrender this to Christ?"*

THE AGREEMENTS WE'VE
MADE ABOUT LOVE

⚶ Okay, I told you we were headed into deeper waters. What did this entry stir in you, the one about love and what we believe about love?

I've also been noticing for sometime now that when I first wake up, I find myself racing through the coming day in my mind, bracing myself for what's required of me, but even more so searching to see if there's anything to look forward to. It's not really voluntary. It's almost as if my heart has a life of its own, and it wakes up before I do and begins to assess the prospects before me. "I slept, but my heart was awake" (Song of Songs 5:2).

By the way, I think this is how our addictions get their claws deeper into us. Our day-to-day grind isn't anything close to Eden, and our hurting and desperate hearts look for something to attach all those yearnings to, and we'll settle for a doughnut if that's all there is to look forward to. We've got to be careful what we give our hearts over to (pages 88–89).

⚶ Do you see something like this playing out in your inner life, this search for something to look forward to?

I know I'm not alone in having a hard time believing in the love of God for me (we think he loves everyone else), or receiving the love of God, or letting it catch my heart up into life and joy, or, maybe especially, *staying* there for any reasonable period of time. An hour or two would be amazing. A day would be a triumph. And I'm thinking, maybe part of the reason hides back in our story somewhere. I remember something Gerald May wrote years ago, that we need to let ourselves tell *our* story of love—how love came to us over the course of our life, or how it did not come, or how it left. We need to tell the story so that we understand. And I remember thinking at the time, *No thank you. I'd rather not go there. Thanks just the same.*

And I ignored it for years.

Now I'm trying to bring my heart back to the love of God, let it heal me, and stay there. It feels sometimes like I'm searching through a dark forest for a wounded deer, and trying to coax it in so I can touch it.

Our story of love is a very tangled story about the most precious thing in our lives (our longing for love). It's a hard story to tell for two reasons. For one thing, we're too close to it to often have any clarity at all. Can't see the forest for the trees. More deeply, it's a heartbreaking story and we're not sure we want to revisit any of that. It's why we're ambivalent about love. Oh, we yearn for it. I want to be loved. But we hide from it, too, build defenses against it, fortress ourselves from being hurt again. We settle for a doughnut.

Then we wonder why it's hard for us to connect with the love of God, let it in so deep it heals us, and remain in his love (pages 90–91).

Clarity

I know we've explored agreements a little bit already, but they are so significant I want to highlight again what I said in this chapter. (This would be one of those lessons-within-the-lesson.) Agreements are really subtle and nasty things. They pin our hearts down, or shut our hearts down, because what they do is hand over to the enemy a sort of key to that room in our hearts, and in *that* place he shuts the door and locks it. This is what's behind the impasses you find in otherwise healthy people's lives. Your friend Jane is a wonderful woman, loves God, leads mission trips. But she collapses internally whenever someone criticizes her. Goes into a depression, and binges. Your brother Dan is a kind and loving man, one of the more mature men you know. But he hasn't returned your calls for three weeks because over dinner one night you asked him why he hasn't been dating anyone.

You've probably just run up against a wounded place in the heart, held in some sort of bondage by an agreement. Quite often having to do with love.

Think back over your story of love. In those moments you've been wounded, that is a really vulnerable time for agreements to come in. They come swiftly, imperceptibly, often as a response to some message delivered with the wound. Your boyfriend breaks up with you. It hurts too much, so you shove the pain down and try to get away from it. But your heart is coming to conclusions. *It's all because of me. I'll never really be loved again.* And the thing is, you may not even be aware that you made the agreement. Our enemy is cunning, and after he secures the agreement he drops the issue for awhile, goes underground, lays low so that nobody discovers his work there. By lays low for a while I mean it could be thirty years or more. All you know is, you can't feel the love of God.

Standing in the bathroom with the shower running and empty, I wonder . . . where, and when did I make the agreement, *I will never be loved?* I wonder . . . how common is that agreement to the human heart?

Jesus, okay. Okay. Come in here. I really want and need your love, much more deeply than I've allowed myself to let it in. I want to stay there, keep my heart in your love. Come and show me what sort of agreements I've made about love. Show me where they are, when they came in. Help me to let them go. Renounce them. Accept your love instead. Oh, heal my fearful heart. I am willing to look at my story of love. Walk with me there (pages 91–92).

What is coming to mind? What do you remember about your story of love, or, what do you hear Jesus saying to you about this?

What do I believe about love?

That it never stays.

Whoa. Geez. How long has that been there? Okay, I see it now. I do not trust love. I don't. That characterizes a lot of my life. *Oh, Jesus, come into this.* Deep sigh. I sit here in silence again for awhile, almost like mourning the delivery of some very sad or somber news. Geez. That is just so sad. I know it's true though, the revelation that is—I do believe that. Doesn't take a brain surgeon to figure out why. Dad left. Alcohol took him away. Mom left. She had to go back to work to support us. Brent left. I realize, at least intellectually, that his death was not really him choosing to walk away from me. But still, he's gone. I could name a number of others, all who left. My life feels like a series of people leaving (pages 92–93).

What do *you* believe about love? Just let your heart answer the question. You may need to repeat the question over to yourself a few times, quietly listening. *What do I believe about love?*

Clarity

I ended this story with the short prayer I prayed before I had to run out the door. But I DO NOT want to give the impression that a short prayer is enough when it comes to the deep things of our hearts. Not at all!

Yes, you do need to ask Jesus what he is saying about all this. And you do need to invite him in. That is how we deal with it *in the moment.*

But you may also need to talk with a friend, or a counselor. You are reading the daily life here of a man who has been through counseling and is himself a counselor. If all this is somewhat new to you, by all means talk to someone about it. I'm showing you how to walk with God through a hundred different scenarios. I don't want to imply that these short entries or "on the fly" prayers are all that is needed for a wounded heart!

The Next Day

That love thing really threw me yesterday. I mean, I wasn't looking to go there. It's such a vulnerable place. My story of love? Good grief . . . it's too much. I just don't want to deal with it, sort through all that. I'd rather keep my distance.

Maybe that's why God has to sneak up on us.

I am so aware—and I see it in all my friends—of this way of living that says, *Don't disrupt me, don't take me into stuff I don't want to deal with. Let me get on with my life.* Remember the Land Cruiser? I don't even want to check the oil, let alone deal with my story of love. *Just let me get on with my life.* And God, in all his loving-kindness, says . . . *No.* (And something in each of us says, *dang.* Or something more colorful. We know it's true. The hound of heaven isn't so easily put off our scent.) God says to us, *We've got to go there. You are not well. Not whole and holy yet, not through and through. I want you to have life, but you won't really have it until you are whole and holy* (pages 93–94).

God has to sneak up on us. He'll use a song we hear on the radio, or an old photograph we happen to see on the wall, he'll use a movie or someone else telling their story to unlock some hidden place in our heart. To draw us back to things we need to deal with.

⚜ Has that happened to you recently? Has something stirred an emotion, or maybe unwelcome tears, has something caught you off guard? What was it? What were the emotions behind it?

⚜ Any hunch of what God might have been "sneaking up" on? Have you asked him?

We walk through the world too vulnerably when we refuse to deal with the deep things of our hearts. Especially our story of love. I told the story of a counseling appointment with a man in a hard marriage. In that story

with us so that he can 4) create a stronghold there.

⚞ Were you aware of this dynamic before I mentioned it?

⚞ Have you just let your emotional life sort of run wild, without considering it might be a dangerous thing to do?

Anyhow, this young man has his grief, but now there's also a spirit of overwhelming sorrow jumping on board and pulling him under. So, he comes by yesterday and asks me if we could talk. I pray with him some, and while I'm praying I am experiencing pain in my own heart. *Oh, so this is what the enemy is doing—he's piercing his heart with sorrow.* I can't begin to number how many times I've experienced this—someone else's spiritual warfare trying to jump on me. The stuff likes to transfer around. Like a computer virus. Just that morning, standing in the bathroom, I was made aware of one of the deep agreements I've made about love, and so I'm a little tender and vulnerable as I go into my day. Now I'm in the arena with a spirit of overwhelming sorrow. Do you see how set up I am to become another victim of this heartache?

If you're not heads up about this stuff, you get mugged.

It would have been easy for the story to have gone on like this: I see in his life that love doesn't work, it doesn't stay, and I could have easily returned to the agreement I'd renounced only that morning. *See, it doesn't. Don't be a fool. You were right all along.* I would have lost the ground gained. And then his warfare is there as well, this spirit of overwhelming sorrow, piercing my heart, assaulting me because I'm trying to help him. If I wasn't aware of how warfare tries to transfer around I could have experienced the heart piercing, thought it was related to my own sorrow, and let it in with the subtle agreement, *Yes, my heart does hurt. Life is sorrow and loss* (pages 94–95).

This is HUGE. If you begin to let this be a category you think in, it will help you immensely. So, who is currently struggling in your life? Who among your friends or family is having a hard time?

Now, when you are with them, or after you are with them, have you noticed the effect on you? What is it?

Have you ever considered that it might be their warfare, jumping on you?

Here's a very helpful way to pray:

"I bring the cross of the Lord Jesus Christ between me and (name the person) and I bring the cross and blood of Jesus Christ against all of their warfare. I (hand) it to hander to (his). I give it no claim in my life. I send it all back, in the name of Jesus Christ."

Do you see what a dangerous world we live in? This is no Sunday school class. This is Vietnam, Kosovo, Baghdad. This is why God is so insistent we deal with the unhealed and unholy places in our lives. He knows how *vulnerable* we are.

Thank God, I had some sense of what was going on. I rejected the lie that his life proved my former agreement about love. Brought the cross of Christ against his warfare and sent it from me to the throne of Christ. And now I am here this morning, out from under all that, and simply back to what God brought up without all the other crap trying to jump on. I am needing to return again to his love, and I feel that what I need right now is just the truth—the objective, everlasting truth about his love for me. So I turn to the Scriptures . . .

I have loved you with an everlasting love;
I have drawn you with loving-kindness.
I will build you up again
and you will be rebuilt . . .
and go out to dance with the joyful. (Jeremiah 31:3–4)

How great is the love the Father has lavished on us, that we should be called children of God! (1 John 3:1)

And hope does not disappoint us, because God has poured out his love into our hearts by the Holy Spirit, whom he has given us. As the Father has loved me, so have I loved you. Now remain in my love. (Romans 5:5)

No, the Father himself loves you because you have loved me and have believed that I came from God. (John 16:27)

I have made you known to them, and will continue to make you known in order that the love you have for me may be in them and that I myself may be in them. (John 17:26)

Let this be true, God says. *Believe it. Make your agreement with me in this.* A beautiful invitation. He knows that we make agreements with all sorts of lies, distortions, accusations, and what not. Now he invites me to agree with him in what is *true.*

We cannot base our convictions on whether or not we are feeling or experiencing the truth of what God says. It is an arrogant posture, to let our immediate state of being be the judge of whether or not the Scripture is true for us. I know I have to start with the truth, embrace it, stake my all on it, and then later— sometimes right away, sometimes down the road—it does shape my experience. Then I experience its truthfulness (pages 95–97).

Linger over these Scriptures for a bit. Let them sink in. Ask Jesus,

"Lord, what are you saying to me? What do you want me to agree with you about?"

What I Have Been

significant issues God raises in my heart. Like the issue of love.

I hope you also see what a beautiful thing it can be to ask Jesus what to pray. Too often we just jump in and start making prayer "speeches" to God. Then we say "amen," leave, and he never gets the chance to speak.

So what I want you to do for a few moments is simply quiet your heart, and ask Jesus, Lord—what should I be praying for myself these days? What should I be praying?

Sit with the question, and repeat is softly to yourself and the Lord, and then listen. What is coming to mind? What do you hear, or sense, or have the impression of?

DREAMS

⟩ The story about mine and Blaine's dream—what did you make of that? What did it stir?

I told this story for three reasons. First, because God does speak to us in *many* different ways, including dreams, and I want you to be open to some new categories of how he might be speaking to you. Too often when some weird "coincidence" happens in our life, we don't do anything with it. We look at it like a two-headed rooster and then go have lunch. BUT, what we can do is walk with God. Ask him. Ask him what it's about. Sometimes it's not about anything (it was just a weird dream, that's all). But sometimes it's meaningful. Walking with God will allow you to sort that out.

Second, I wanted to underscore this idea of asking God how to pray. This is a BIGGIE. One of the really big lessons-within-the-lesson.

What do I pray, Lord? What is this about?

Pause. This is a really, really helpful place to begin—to ask God what to pray. I don't know what's going on. I'm looking at the equivalent of a two-headed rooster on my windowsill. I don't know why God brought this up. So I ask him. Remember the disciples—they said to Jesus, "Teach us to pray." Too many times we just jump in and start praying (making prayer speeches to God) and it doesn't have much effect. We just sort of swing our sword around in the air randomly. Do this for awhile and you'll get the impression that prayer doesn't really work. Or that God isn't really in it. Oh, it works, and he's in it. When we pray effectively. John says,

> This is the confidence we have in approaching God, that if we ask anything according to his will, he hears us. And if we know that he hears us—whatever we ask—we know that we have what we asked of him. (1 John 5:14–15)

That's an awesome promise. If we pray according to God's will, he hears us alright. And he answers our prayers. Isn't that what you want? I sure do. I want to see my prayers work! I want to pray according to the will of God. But I don't always know what that is. So, *I ask*. This has absolutely revolutionized the way I pray. And I am seeing a lot more results, just as the Scripture promised.

This really has changed the way I pray. Give it a try.

Third, I wanted to put in your quiver this understanding of spiritual authority.

In order to understand the dynamic here, you need to understand something about spiritual authority. When you place yourself under a church (by joining it), or under a company (by taking employment there), you come under their spiritual authority. This can be good, and it can be bad. It depends upon what the leaders choose to let in, spiritually speaking.

People coming out of cults often struggle with spiritual oppression until they sever all spiritual bonds with that cult and its leaders. Sadly, if an otherwise good church has given place to a strong spirit of religious pride, then you'll often find that most of its members struggle with religious pride. It goes around, infects everybody like the flu. The same dynamic holds true in families. Have you ever wondered why adultery or divorce or financial ruin seems to run in certain families? Because somewhere along the line the leader of that family let it in, through their own sins and agreements, and it passes down the line until someone takes a stand against it (pages 103–104).

Does this raise any thoughts for you? Any connections in your own life?

The best thing to do at this point is what I did (I hope you are not getting tired of me saying this): ask God! *What do I pray Lord?*

But I also include this prayer, because it might help:

"I bring the full work of my Lord Jesus Christ—his cross and shed blood, his resurrection and his life, his authority, rule and dominion—between me and (this place—who they were doesn't matter for the story, and I am not impugning them in any way), and between me and all the people there. Its officers and leadership, and my former boss. I sever all spiritual ties between us, and I cancel any claims the enemy is making to me now because of my time spent there. I come out from under their authority. I consecrate my calling and my gifting to God. I cleanse my calling and gifting with the blood of Jesus Christ, to be holy and pure and filled with the Spirit of God alone. I keep the work of Christ between us, and forbid these ties to be reformed. In the Name and the authority of the Lord Jesus Christ (page 104)."

This is one of the most beautiful fruits of learning to hear the voice of God—offering to pray and listen for someone else. I could have told, literally, a thousand stories of our fellowship offering this to one another—and to perfect strangers!

> Sally came to me a few days ago, tears in her eyes, dark circles from lack of sleep. "I don't know what to do," she said. Now, I've noticed over the years that I have two reactions when someone is in distress. I feel uncomfortable, and want to get beyond the awkwardness as quickly as possible. This is what fuels our attempts to offer a quick word of comfort, or advice, hoping to shift the conversation or get out of the room as quick as we can. It's god-less. It's cowardice. It is nothing less than retreat—a retreat from

battles we don't know we can handle, don't *want* to handle, a retreat to try and get back to a nice little life as quick as we can (pages 105–106).

How do you normally react when someone is in distress?

Thank God, there is another response that's been growing in me over time, growing as Jesus comes to have more and more of me. I want to engage. I want to intervene. I want to help. I asked Sally what she felt was going on, wanted to hear her perspective on her distress. Was she aware that it seemed way out of proportion? Was she aware that this had one part to do with the young man and five parts to do with deeper issues in her soul? After all, when it comes to helping another human being, you can treat the symptoms or you can treat the cause. Most people dabble in symptom management, and that is why most people don't seem to be getting better. (page 106)

In your "Christian world," the orbit of your Christian fellowship, do folks typically treat the symptom or the cause?

Are people getting better?

A bit more on the dynamics of helping someone. In addition to having an eye out for what is going on in their heart, you have to have your radar up for what the enemy is doing as well. Sally's friends were mostly irritated with her, the result being they were

The night before the day of intervention, I had a crappy night of sleep. That's a good sign—the enemy is freaking out, knows his gig is up, and now the warfare is transferring to you. Don't let that deter you, either. Take it as a sign that something good is going to happen. Breakthrough is on the way (page 107).

This will be very helpful to keep in mind—the enemy is always trying to get you to do to people what he is trying to do to them. So, try this—list a few people you are close to, and then, try and name what you "feel" when you're round them. For example, your brother is Jeremy, and what you feel around him is, "He kinda bugs me, I want to dismiss him." There you go—you just identified what I am talking about.

What was so sweet about the time of prayer was that several of us could listen and pray on Sally's behalf. *We* could hear the voice of God when she could not. But as we prayed over each thing Christ revealed, Sally began to come back to her true self. And she began to hear the voice of God. Oh, how I wish this was more widely practiced in the body of Christ. One of the richest treasures of learning to hear God's voice is the great good we can do for others. In fact, I think you'll find that listening for others will develop your ability to hear for yourself (page 108).

If you haven't yet, give this a try—begin to offer to listen on someone else's behalf. Somebody drops by your office and they tell you a story of not being able to know God's direction. Offer to pray with them, introduce to them the whole idea of listening. (What usually happens is the other person jumps in and starts making a prayer speech. When they've finished, say, "Now let's simply be quiet and ask Jesus what he wants to say to us.") It will be a great blessing.

RETALIATION

Did the story about the day after helping Sally make sense? What struck you about the idea of retaliation?

What I was hit with, right there in the phone call, was, *I give up. This kind of prayer doesn't work. Forget it. God doesn't come through for people, healing doesn't really happen. Just back away from people.* Subtle, but clear. An agreement with the very warfare this poor woman had been making agreements with herself. Desolation. After I hang up I have to renounce this. "No," I say out loud. "That is not true. I reject that feeling (it often comes as a feeling) and I reject that lie. God is at work (page 109)."

This is far more common than most people know. Think about someone you're trying to help, or simply love, or maybe share the gospel with. What do you experience every time you try?

There are a couple of things to learn from this. The first is, don't just assume the attack you are under on any given day is yours. It might be someone else's battle, trying to transfer to you. Sometimes it happens after you've been a help to them, and sometimes it comes *beforehand*, trying to take you out so that you don't even offer any help. Let this be a category for you, when you realize you are under some form of attack—*Where is this coming from? Whose warfare might this be?* Ask God about it.

We will be pressed, when we are helping others, to succumb to whatever it is that besets them. "Brothers," Paul says, "if someone is caught in a sin, you who are spiritual should restore him gently. But watch yourself, or you also may be tempted" (Galatians 6:1). The enemy will try to find a weakness—an old wound, an agreement, some fear or sin—in order to get you to give way, so that you cannot help the person in need. As we are being pressed, we have an immediate opportunity to break any agreements we've made, repent of any sins we've committed, so that we might be whole and holy, so that we might help those we love. I find I have to do this in the moment, in the midst of the conversation or the prayer. *Lord, I've done the same thing. Forgive me. Cleanse me. I renounce the agreements I've made here* (pages 109–110).

> Have you seen this at work in your life? Can you see now how important it is not to give way to their "stuff," and NOT to make an agreement with it yourself?

We might not always be able to rouse ourselves to fight the battle on our own behalf. But we may find a deeper resolve when it comes to loving others. Don't give way, don't surrender. You are needed (page 110).

> You are needed. What does that stir in you?

BACK TO JOY

> Do you begin to see now how essential joy is?

Because we live in a world at war. *Because* the enemy is relentless. *Because* we are "hard pressed on every side" (2 Corinthians 4:8). For this very reason we need joy. Lots and lots of joy. Bucketfuls.

twisted, diminished version of battle and joy. Push hard, and then reward yourself with a little something. Work like a dog and then buy yourself a big screen TV. It's a cheap counterfeit of battle and a cheap counterfeit of joy.

If you would walk with God you will find yourself called up to the real thing. Intense battle. Authentic joy. But the battle will find you. I think we have to be intentional about the joy (pages 110–111).

So, how can you be intentional about joy this week? This month? What will you do? Write out here a plan to go get some joy. It might be seeing a movie with a friend, or taking a day off, or making a trip you've been wanting to take for some time. What's your plan for joy?

The Spirit of the Age

I hate the pace of my life. I don't live. I get things done. My life is entirely task-oriented. I wake and pray, because if I don't pray, I get taken out by warfare. But it's not leisurely prayer, it's purposeful prayer. I head to the office, and start replying to emails. Projects that began with a good idea are now breathing down my neck because there are deadlines to these things and what began as a creative outburst is now just Get It Done. I come home exhausted, fried, and that's where the drinking thing turned sour. Sometimes I'll try to get a run in—but did you notice the phrase, "get it in?" Another get it done. Even though I do enjoy running, it's become fit it in. Task, not living.

I used to enjoy asking people "How are you?" Now I avoid the question, because it's an invitation to a conversation I don't have time for, and, it's going to take us into issues I am going to feel obligated to do something about. I mean, when they say "Not so good," where do we go from there? "Oh, I'm sorry. Well, gotta go." So I'm trying not to ask the question, so I can go on with my day and get things done (page 112).

Can you relate? Do you see this at work in your life? How?

Every age has a certain spirit or mood or climate to it. Ours is Busyness. We're all of us running like lemmings from sunup to way past sundown. We are running around like ants do when you kick in their hill, like rats on a wheel, like Carroll's Mad Hatter.

And for some reason, we either believe we can't stop or we don't want to (pages 113–114).

Right? Have you fallen to believing that—that there is nothing you can do about the pace of your life? (Have you done anything about it?)

Like the prodigal son, we are not going to do a thing about this until we wake one day to realize we are sick of it, *and we want a different life.* Till then, the life of not living but getting things done has its benefits. For one, it provides us with an illusion of security—I am tackling life, I am staying on top of things. It's a false security, but we don't believe that. We believe it's our only road to security. Stay on top of things. We might not be so honest as to say, *God doesn't seem particularly involved in taking care of these things for me, so I have to do it.* But it's our underlying conviction. After all, if we believed God was going to take care of all that concerns us, we wouldn't kill ourselves trying to hold our world up (page 113).

This sort of honesty and confession is so very important if we would move toward God and the life he wants us to live. How does your busyness and the things you are committed to, how do they give you a sense of security? (Maybe the quickest way to find that out is to ask, what do you feel about letting it all go? Stopping?)

> Then there is the wonderful quality of the endless distraction it provides. But it's "purposeful distraction." I don't have to face myself, or God, or anyone else because I'm so very busy. And the bonus is, I don't have to feel guilty that I'm not facing myself, or God, or anyone else because my busyness is "just the way it is," and by golly at least I'm showing I'm a responsible person by getting things done. Thus I can avoid any real disruption while feeling the victim of circumstances beyond my control (pages 113–114).

And the distraction—can you see how part of you enjoys it, uses it to avoid deeper things?

If we really wanted to live differently you would see some sign of that in our choices.

Just let that sink in for a moment. If you really wanted to live differently you would see some sign of that in your choices. What are you moved to do?

Hawks

I talked about how God has been speaking to me through hawks. And how God is speaking to us all the time. Sometimes he uses words. Other times he uses dreams. And he loves to use the ever changing, unfolding beauty, drama and presence of his creation.

> Thanks to the human heart by which we live,
> Thanks to its tenderness, its joys, and fears,
> To me the meanest flower that blows can give
> Thoughts that do often lie too deep for tears (page 115).

How has God been speaking to you, other than through his Word, or through the grace of hearing his voice? Have you noticed him speaking to you through some aspect of his creation?

Winter

Finding God in Our Losses, in the Mundane, and Sustaining Our Hearts Over What Can Feel Like the Long Path of Obedience

THE PASSING OF SCOUT

☙ What did the story of Scout's passing stir in you?

☙ Scout's death was hard for our family. We all suffer loss and in this story the key issue is to walk with God in loss, and to ask him how to handle it, what to pray for. What losses have you experienced most recently?

☙ And were you able to find God in the midst of that?

How important this is—to be willing to hear whatever it is God wants to say. Have you been having a hard time hearing from God? On what issue?

Are you open to hearing whatever it is he wants to say?

GOD IN OUR LOSS

Scout's passing was the hardest, most beautiful thing we've yet shared with our boys, except for the loss of my dear friend Brent, eight years ago. In our grief we *need* the comfort and care that only God can bring. When, in what circumstances, have you *known* God cares for your heart?

What do you typically do when sorrow comes—do you find yourself walking with God?

I cannot tell you how much I wanted to be able to pray and heal Scout. But you have to be *so* careful with your heart and your faith when it comes to healing prayer. It's *so* important to know what God is up to. When the disciples asked Jesus about a man born blind, Jesus said the man had been born blind so that the work of God could be displayed in his life (John 9). And right then and there he healed him. But there were a lot of blind people in Israel at that time whom Jesus *didn't* heal. So a few weeks ago I began to ask, *Jesus, do you want to heal Scout? Is that what you want to do here?* I sensed the answer was *No. Not this time.*

In learning to hear the voice of God, one thing is certain—if you cannot hear a "no," you will have a hard time hearing God at all or believing that what you think you've heard is in fact from God. This is crucial—hearing God requires surrender, giving all things over into his hands. Not abandoning your desires, but yielding them to God. Of course I wanted to hear Jesus say, *Yes, I will heal him.* I wanted to hear that so badly. Then I would have gone after healing prayer like a man on a mission. I would have prayed like Elijah. But I could not do that to my family unless I knew God was fully in it. I didn't want to drag them through that (*Walking with God*, pages 118–119).

Maybe what you need to do is walk with God *now*, through former losses. Ask him about it—not demanding an explanation—but rather, ask him to speak to you about it, to comfort you. Invite him into it. Process it now, with him.

Now, I don't know what you are going to make of this, but I

stop there? Many good theologians believe we will see our beloved animals in heaven. But I won't go into a theological debate here. I asked Jesus, *What do dogs do in the kingdom, Lord?* And he said, *They run.* And then I saw Scout, with the eyes of my heart, running with a whole pack of very happy dogs, near the feet of Jesus.

I shared the story with Stasi and the boys, and Blaine said, "Yes. I heard something too. Right after Scout died. Jesus said, *'He won't give me the ball.'* " That was Scout's trademark, to come up to you to play ball, tennis ball already in his mouth, but then he wouldn't give it to you. To hear that from Jesus was more precious to us than I can say.

We buried Scout in the backyard, up the hill in the scrub oak. I'd gone out there the day before to dig the hole. There, lying on the spot I'd chosen, was a small granite stone about the size of your hand, but in the shape of a heart. I kept it, and when we buried Scout I showed it to Stasi and the boys. Another gift from God. He cares about our hearts (pages 121–122).

＊ Can you describe the words, gifts or provision that have expressed God's comfort and care in your loss? What did he say, or how did he show you he cared?

＊ God's heart is to bring comfort to us in our loss/grief/pain . . . we often miss it looking elsewhere. Where do you normally go for the comfort you need?

ACCEPT THE GRACE GOD IS GIVING

＊ As you read the continuation of our experience of God being so *present and kind* in the midst of our loss there may be a couple of things that leap off these pages. What is God saying to you right now though our story?

Would you expect God to come for you?

I was afraid of Scout's death, afraid of the grief, because when I lost Brent years ago, it was the most excruciating thing I'd ever gone through. I was afraid that this grief would open the door to that one. Sorrow is like that—it seems connected to all the other sorrows in your life. Like opening the door into a room where all your sorrow is stored. But it didn't happen. There are echoes of Brent's death, but this time I feel different. A lot different.

It's as if I'm substantially healed. Wow. Healing really does take place. And there is another thing. When I said good-bye to Scout, I also said, "I'll see you again, boy." It resolved something in my soul. Our losses are not permanent, not when they are in the hands of God. What a difference that makes (page 122).

Oh, it's true, there is healing. There is comfort . . . our losses are not permanent!

🌿 I saw how I could miss the healing and comfort God has for me by making a very natural agreement that "I *ought to* feel bad" given my losses. Have you found yourself in some way choosing pain and grief over comfort and healing?

I've noticed that Jesus is offering comfort and well-being to me today. But I also notice that I have a choice whether to accept them. It almost seems wrong to be feeling okay only days after Scout's death and all that our family went through. Like it somehow diminishes what he meant to me, the sadness of his death, the loss, and especially it somehow diminishes what the others are feeling, because they are not doing well. It's almost a version of survivor's guilt, that thought that says, *I shouldn't be doing well, look at the others.*

Be careful of this. "I ought to feel bad" can quickly become an agreement with feeling bad, and it shouldn't then come as a surprise that pretty soon you start feeling bad. My goodness—

see your losses, and especially, how you might experience them?

What grief or loss do you need to invite God into?

THE DEVIL IS AN OPPORTUNIST

Have you noticed how quickly things can change in your emotions? I'm feeling good. Enjoying life and communion with Christ and *then* a heaviness begins to creep over me. We are at war. We have an adversary. And he is an Opportunist.

⫸ When during this last week or month have you been aware of the devil trying to find a vulnerability in you, a window of opportunity, an open door or a chink in your armor to spin his lies, deceits and oppression? Can you see now that he might have been trying to "ride in" on the coattails of some event or struggle of yours?

⫸ What are the messages or lies he would love to have you believe about life, God, yourself?

It's great that you caught it! But can you imagine now the number of times, over the years, you weren't aware of his schemes? I'm amazed at how often I need to be reminded that our adversary is a predator and

We must be aware of this—Satan is an opportunist.

He is always looking for open doors, opportunities, a chink in the armor. He'll seize what might otherwise simply be an event—an argument, an emotion, a loss like this—and he'll use it as an entrée for his lies, deceits, and oppression. I've felt it around someone else's bad news. I'll be doing fine, and then someone will tell me a story of some hardship or loss that a friend is undergoing, and *boom*—a sense of lingering darkness will creep over me, not strong at first, just that sense of, *Right, this is what life is really like—it's hard and unpredictable.* It feels like an assault against my faith. Sure, some of this is my own weirdness and paranoia. But not all of it.

What I'm warning you about is that when you are in a vulnerable place, realize that you are in a vulnerable place, and remember that all predators look for the vulnerable one in the herd. Once we are in the kingdom that is yet to come, once the world has been restored to all it was meant to be, then we will be able to live without interruption, without assault. Then we can drop our guard. But not until then. Not even in moments of tenderness and sorrow. I know it seems unfair, but the enemy does not play fair. He is an opportunist (pages 124, 126).

☙ As you walk with God you'll develop a biblical worldview (you'll have to!) and with that comes less hesitancy in identifying the Opportunist's schemes. And a quicker response of effective prayer. Is anything keeping you from fully embracing these realities?

☙ Is there something you need to ask Jesus about here?

It might be as simple as, "Lord Jesus, please give me eyes to see when I am being attacked. And give me the courage to face it, and deal with it.

[illegible blurred text]

it comes to relating to the people in your life?

Our tendency is to go with whatever it is we're feeling. It is not a reliable guide. We run with the speculation, or the worry, guilt, or sense of obligation. Or we give way to the irritation, the, malaise, or the desire to write them off. We find ourselves over-committed or entangled in their drama. Then we resent people as a category because we're spent. And the reason?

We never asked God about it.

Pause right now. Ask God what he is saying about the people you are currently worrying about, or concerned for, or obsessing over.

. . . More often than any other guidance, what I hear God saying to me when I ask about a person is, *Give them to me.*

This response has been consistently counterintuitive, and utterly refreshing
(page 128).

⚓ Why is it hard to surrender relationships to the God who says, "*Give
them to me*"?

⚓ Are you willing to give them to God now?

THE SNARE OF SPECULATION

⚓ As you read through this entry, what occurred to you?

hopeful? What does that tell you?

I began to notice that my imagination just takes off on a whim with all sorts of scenarios during the course of a day. Stasi mentions that someone's child has left the faith, and I immediately go to, *Wow, that could happen to us. Is it Blaine? Sam? Luke?* I start imagining the possibilities. We have a bad month financially, and I run with the thought, *We're going to end up living under a bridge.* The truck makes a thumping noise when I start it, and my imagination jumps to *The engine's going. I'd better sell it before it implodes.* I can already see it up on blocks in front of the house.

The speculation thing was happening a lot in my relationships. Leigh misses one of our church meetings, and I think, *She's drifting away. We're losing her. Any day now she'll be gone.* All she was doing was visiting a friend. Morgan sends an e-mail,

Winter

"Can I talk to you?" and I think, *He's going down. Something's gone wrong. It's probably a meltdown in the events department.* Turns out he had a question about a book. Gary skips a staff meeting, and I jump to *What—we're not a priority? He thinks he can just come and go as he pleases? What an arrogant way to live.* He had a doctor's appointment. This speculation is devastating to relationships, and mine was running rampant (page 130).

Who have you been speculating about recently? What fruit does it bear? It might be good to stop and pray about that now. Renounce the speculation, specifically, person by person. Release them to God. Trust them to God.

The other category of speculation I confessed was doing even more damage to my soul—worrying about my holiness, looking for something wrong in my life.

Now, if you begin to introduce uncertainty in your soul with the search for something wrong there, under the conviction, *Something's wrong,* well guess what—you'll soon find yourself in distress, because something *is* wrong. What's wrong is that I am no longer trusting God. I've moved out of the restful posture of faith and assurance, and that *is* wrong (unbelief and mistrust are wrong). My soul begins to manifest the signs of *something's wrong.*

But the sad irony is I don't notice what's really wrong—the fact
that I'm operating out of fear and mistrust—because I'm looking
for something else, some sin I'm afraid I've committed, some turn

꧁ Our imagination is such an important part of our being . . . shaping
and influencing our every day, our every relationship. Is your imagination an area to sanctify to the lordship of Jesus Christ?

IT WILL COME AROUND

There's a lesson-within-the-lesson that we first need to grab here—the idea
of listening to God as a way of leading a church or ministry or organization.

This would be a tremendous source of guidance and relief if the leaders of churches, ministries and businesses would adopt this approach in their day-to-day decision making. Ask God. Listen for his voice. Together. Surrender to what you hear. Think of all the foolish things that would be avoided, and all the noble things God has for us to embrace. It's an act of humility, really, by which we admit we haven't the smarts to run this thing and we need the counsel of God. In the small things as much as the big ones (page 133).

Is this how your church, ministry or company makes decisions? If not, why not?

At the heart of *Walking with God* is the humility on our part to simply turn and listen to God. We really, really need his counsel. *In the small things as much as the big ones.* Living in community really proves this true.

You see, whenever we live in relationship, whenever we simply live in *proximity* to other people, sooner or later we will run up against their issues—the unhealed or unholy parts of their personalities. Just as they will run into ours. Living in community is like a pack of porcupines sharing the same den. We will get stuck. And the question presses in, *What do I do with that?*

Ask God (page 134).

Be honest, isn't one of the most difficult things about walking with God having to relate to imperfect and at times difficult people? There are so many books offering tips and insight into relationships, interpersonal communica-

Walk with God. *When do I bring this up, Lord? What do I say?* And wait for the go-ahead, even if it means months or years. It will take real restraint. Genuine holiness. But what you can rest assured in is this—the issue will come around again. This isn't the only chance you'll have. Pray as soon as you encounter it, but be willing to let it go, no matter how tweaked you are, if that's what God says to do. It will come around again.

"There is a time for everything," Solomon reminds us, "and a season for every activity under heaven . . . a time to be silent and a time to speak" (Ecclesiastes 3:1, 7). I'm just not wise enough or compassionate enough or brave enough or gentle enough to always discern if this is the time to venture into someone else's life. So I ask God. And wait. It will come around (pages 134–135).

There's a difference between a godly restraint and a passive disengagement in dealing with relational issues. What's your usual style and timeline for dealing with the conflict, hurts, dismissals, and offenses with those in your community?

Do you see that walking with God is a posture of asking, *"Is this the time"* in going after another person's issues. What difference would this make in your life?

Who are the people you need to give to God and trust that these issues that do need to be dealt with *will* come around again?

This is another one of those "Biggies." Practice this, and you will be so free!

In You

There is often a disparity between *our* perception of how we're doing *and* how God thinks we're doing. Go with this for a moment, it will do you great good. Write down right now how you think you're doing in life. Then ask Jesus, How do I think I'm doing, because sometimes we don't even know what we believe about ourselves. Write that down, too.

Then ask him, and how do you think I'm doing, Lord? This might be a harder one to hear, because we are so used to living under guilt and accusation, or a false sense of security, it can be hard to hear on this one. Stay with it. Ask him to speak. Write that down.

If you go to God with a question . . . he will answer. Sometimes God's response to us totally catches us off guard. God's response totally caught me off guard. What did you hear? Did you hear something you didn't expect?

His line of approach caught me off guard and took me straight to the heart of the issue. Here's how it worked. I had been trying really hard to be a good dad. To live a life of genuine integrity. To walk with God. Truth is, I was worn out from trying so hard and was feeling like I was just barely making it. When he said, *I am in you,* suddenly, with that clarity only the Holy Spirit gives, it was clear to me that it is *his* life in me that is supposed to be my hope of being a good dad and a good man, of walking well with him. All in a moment I was aware that my hopes had somehow shifted to my integrity and my ability to self-discipline and self-motivate. To endure. To make it happen (page 138).

Has Christ given you words that left you puzzled about their meaning?

It may be two weeks later, it may be two months or longer, but know that his heart *is* for you, to speak clearly. And it can take time to get clarity. In the rush of life we may not stay with the mystery of all God is saying. But try what I did—write down what you do have—the questions, or the fragments of God speaking—and stay with it. Pursue him with your desire for clarity. *"What's that mean? I don't get it God . . . say more here".*

What clarity about your life and relationship with God are you seeking currently?

The Power of the Right Word

When Jesus said to me on the beach in Mexico, *Just barely,* I was first struck by the brevity of the phrase. And by the freshness of it. I hadn't been using it. But it was right on. A bull's-eye. A perfect phrase for what I was believing but didn't know I was believing, and it also had the quality of haunting me. It unnerved me. I didn't like it. But I knew immediately that it was true. And it was the kind of expression I could hang on to without a pen or journal nearby, could hang on to for several days in the wilderness until I did get to a place where I could write it down and give it some more thought.

Wasn't that both kind and effective?

That's why I have found it so rich to ask Jesus what he is saying to us. For he knows the very words we need to hear. What he will say to me is exactly what my heart needs to hear, will be the very words that best convey his meaning to my heart with greatest precision. He may speak to you on the very same subject, but he will choose the words that are best for you to get his meaning and spirit across. For he knows us, and he wants us to understand not just what he says but what he *means* and the spirit of his meaning.

Just barely and *In you* was exactly what I needed to hear. The words pierced, exposed, comforted, and intrigued me to seek more, all at the same time. That is the beauty of asking God what his word to us is, personally (pages 139–140, 143).

And so as you are moving through your day and week, ask God what he is saying to you—about this relationship, or about work, about your need for joy. Practice asking.

It is very helpful to realize that words and phrases carry a certain meaning and spirit to us. Because there are certain phrases that will open up our hearts to the meaning God intended, and there are words and phrases that *close* our hearts to his meaning. I noticed this during my years of counseling, how a simple turn of a phrase or different choices of words would suddenly open up someone's heart and they'd be weeping over an issue we'd spent months talking about and now, with the right choice of words, the truth had finally struck home. Sunk in. Reached them where it mattered (page 142).

this operating in your Christian world?

And when we come up against a religious word or phrase in our reading or in some religious context, no matter how precious it may be to a certain translation or body of believers, if it conveys a meaning and a spirit other than the meaning and spirit of Jesus Christ, then we must reject it. We do not worship language, we worship the *living* God, who assures us that his word to us is life (John 6:63) (page 143).

This will help you to sort through all those Christian books and movements out there. You shall know them by their fruit. Take something you've encountered recently—a book, a sermon, a Christian ministry. Test it. Does it draw you to God—*really*? Does it sound right because it sounds religious, or does it produce the freedom and life and intimacy with God the Scriptures are intended to produce?

THINGS THAT GO BUMP IN THE NIGHT

⚓ Okay, the sleep story and prayer—what did you make of that?

⚓ There's several lessons in this story. The first isn't so much about sleep, but rather thinking in the category of something important being stolen, and realizing it isn't "just the way life goes" but that the thief is doing it! Do you think like this about the stolen things in your life right now?

You're probably going to start waking up at 4:30 a lot. It just comes with getting older. And it's not so bad really. You can live with that. Geez, flippin' Louise. These guys just don't quit. If I begin to make that agreement, guess what's going to happen—I *am* going to start to wake at 4:30 consistently, and I'm going to accept it as just part of growing older and never see the thief behind my stolen rest (page 144).

⚹ What might you be surrendering right now through a habit or mindset

I share the prayer that Stasi and I have been praying now most evenings prior to our sleep. What in the Bedtime Prayer is new to you? Are you willing to try it for a season?

⚹ In the beginning of the prayer we address our need to be restored and renewed in Christ. At the end of most days aren't you needing a bit of restoration and renewal? How's the thought of ending your day asking God to restore and renew you instead of simply letting exhaustion, anxiety, or anger be the primary reality of day's end?

⟋ Next we bring the full work of Christ between ourselves and everyone we've been with throughout the day. We compare the dynamic of other people's warfare *"jumping"* upon us as a computer virus-like effect. Have you experienced the computer virus-like effect of other people's warfare?

⟋ In the past how have you dealt with it?

> As I pray this I listen to God, letting him bring people to mind, for I may specifically need to bring the cross of Christ between us. I'll completely forget that only four hours ago I was counseling someone battling suicidal thoughts and depression, and I sure don't want that stuff around here tonight. Then I bring the work of Christ against all witchcraft. Pagan rites and rituals are back in force these days, and there's a lot of witchcraft raised against the church—curses, rituals, stuff like that. The culture we live in now is like Egypt or Babylon of the Old Testament. Bizarre is in. Demonic is in. But it's nothing to get freaked out about—it's no different than what any modern missionary in Brazil or Uganda has to deal with (page 147).

In the spiritual realm do you *really* think we're exempt from the realities we find easier to accept as unfolding in the dark far-reaching corners of the globe?

Naming them has proven important. Adam was given authority to name things, and in doing so he exercised a sort of authority over them. The principle holds here. You're dealing with twisted beings who have no intention of yielding. The more specific and direct you can be, the better (see Mark 5:1–13) (page 148).

You see that this requires *intentionality*, and that is the point. God wants us to rise up, and be intentional. Don't just fluff up the pillow and try to ignore it. Deal with these guys!

Yes, it's a hassle to do this. Especially when you get home late and all you want to do is fall into bed. Yes, you won't want to do it every night for months and years. I have friends who struggle with their sleep but won't pray about it. I understand. There are lots of nights I wish I didn't have to. But it's worth it. For one, you'll get a good part of your sleep back. Maybe all of it. But for another, it will make you holy. To come to Christ and realign yourself with him at the end of your day when you *are* utterly spent and *don't* want to pray has a deeply sanctifying effect (page 149).

Winter

121

How many of your decisions about, and your "theology" about spiritual warfare is simply driven by the fact that it's a hassle and you'd really rather not deal with it?

Would you do it if it made a difference?

So when do you start?

ACHING

Do you ever catch yourself daydreaming? About what?

Pushing a little deeper, is there anything you are looking forward to right now?

This side of heaven we all ache for something, what did you realize in reading this that you ache for?

I feel like I'm skirting around the edge of some mountainous issue. I feel as if the way I live is just "keeping life from going bad." Push hard, get it done, come through, because no one else will. *Endure.* I underestimate my willingness to endure. This feels like the source of my ache. I put my head in my hands for a long time. This is the one quality I think I like most about myself, feel most noble about—my willingness to endure. And yet I think it has become something other than noble. Perhaps even something destructive.

I know I'm onto something huge here. There is little room for joy in my life when I'm living like this. There isn't much room for joy in Endure. I'm trying to sort this out. Where did it come from? Is it sin? Woundedness? How deep does this run in me? I think there is a lot of unbelief behind Endure, like my conviction that no one else is going to come through, so I have to. It also feels like Samson's downfall—we find a quality or a strength that helps us get through life, and we make it our idol, put all our trust and hope in it.

But once we make this strength or quality an idol and turn to it for security, it becomes our blind spot—the thing we don't want anyone to look at or tamper with. Not even God. Eventually it becomes our ruin (pages 150–152).

Earlier in our journey through this Guide we talked about our basic approach to life (mine was "attack the day, get it done"). We find a way of making life work. Were you able to name yours at the time? Can you name it now? Do you see it more clearly these days?

don't let anyone get close." And then you ache, because you are made for love and no one can get close to love you. Ask Jesus to shed light on how your approach to life is hurting you.

Jesus, I don't want to say this is the unapproachable subject. You can speak to me here, about this. I want you to. I invite you to.

MOTIVE

What's your gut reaction to this entry on motives—and how even our personality has a motive behind it?

Within the Christian community we tend to focus on behavior, and that is right and that is wrong. Of course what we do matters. It matters how you treat people. It matters whether or not you lie or steal or commit adultery. Our actions have enormous consequences to them. However, according to Jesus, holiness is a matter of the heart. This is the gist of his famous Sermon on the Mount. Jesus says, why do you pray? To be seen as holy? Why do you give? To be seen as generous? Why do you fast? To impress others (page 152)?

Motive is an essential category in learning to walk with God. As you listen for his voice you also want to be aware of your motives with a basic question, *"What's going on inside?"* Our motive is very basic to our pursuit of God, and the transformation he is always after in our lives—everything we do has a reason behind it, a motive.

In your Christian walk how important has reflection upon the motives beneath your behaviors been?

Now, what most people don't realize is that what we call our personality has some very deep and profound motives behind it as well. Call it your approach to life. Have you ever asked yourself what's behind it? As I've already shared, I can be a very driven man. Part of that comes out of some childhood wounds. I found myself on my own. But part of it comes out of my sinful response to those wounds—my resolution to make it on my own. I won't need anyone. Not even God. Some of you are always friendly. (I can't seem to pull that one off.) Is it just your natural buoy-

How would you describe your personality?

Has it ever occurred to you that it has a motive behind it? Would you be willing to look at what motives might lay beneath your personality?

I know men who say they're just not comfortable in the out-doors—they don't go for all that outdoor stuff. Now, that may be a matter of preference—but how does that work for them? Perhaps they don't want to be tested and exposed. Perhaps it's fear of not really being a man that keeps them at home. I hear women say, "I'm not into all that women's stuff, dresses and beauty and all that." It might be true. It might be that they're more of the tomboy sort. Then again, how does that work for them? Are they able to avoid facing issues of insecurity, doubts about their femininity (page 154)?

What do you suspect is a motive explaining so much of your personality? Another way you might answer this is, what do you fear people will say about you if they *really* know you?

Now, I am not saying this to usher in waves of self-reproach and despair. "I'm a disaster. I'm a nightmare of twisted motives. Who even knows all that's going on down in there? Whatever is not from faith is sin??? My whole approach to life is suspect." Probably. Take a number. It's true for the rest of us as well. That's okay. You are forgiven. God has been well aware of this for years, and he's still been right there with you. Isn't he gracious, and patient? But now you have the opportunity to be transformed in some really genuine ways (page 155).

You are known, and you are loved. Right now. Where you are. In that security, you can be open to what God is trying to get at in your motives. Do you have a hunch what he is after these days? Ask him!

HEALING THE PAST

This is one of the most beautiful aspects of Christianity, and one of the least understood. God really does want to heal us. Make us whole and holy, remember?

ing with Jesus, we can invite him into our past and walk with him there too. Much of our hearts were shaped "back then," most of our deep convictions formed. Oh, how I wish I had been a Christian in high school, walked with God during those years. But I did not, and I am asking Christ back into those events and relationships as memories surface—or, when something like this party stirs longings familiar to those I felt then (page 157).

Where have you been feeling uncomfortable lately? At a party or a gathering? At work? What emotions have been surfacing that you don't really know what to do with?

Ask Jesus what it's about. Invite him in. and while you do, answer this question—"When have I felt like this before?" Think back over your life—you'll see a theme. Every time someone tries to get close, or every time you fear someone is leaving, or whenever you are criticized, you feel like this. You're getting to the past that needs to be healed.

Ask Jesus to reveal to you where it all got started for you. As I'm processing and praying about my dislike of being the center of attention at parties, Jesus begins to expose something larger and deeper than my social anxiety. I see a pattern of seeking transcendence in some pretty dark places that goes back to my high school years.

> As I was praying about all this, I began to ask forgiveness for the things that happened during those years. I wasn't repenting of my search for joy, but of the places I let it take me. I found myself then praying against despair as the deeper issue. Let me explain. I didn't grow up in a Christian home. My dad went through some hard years of unemployment and fell to drinking. My mom went back to work. By the time I was in high school, my family had fallen apart. As I was praying about those years, I began to see how the collapse at home sent me on this search. It's as if, having made an agreement with despair, I turned to those parties to get high and make out with girls, grasping to fill the ache with something.
>
> I sensed Jesus saying, *Renounce the despair.* So I did. *Renounce turning to women and sexual sin.* So I did. *And turning to drugs and alcohol.* I prayed, *Oh, Jesus, I do, I renounce it all. I ask your forgiveness. Cleanse me. Come back into those years with me and sanctify my heart* (pages 156–157).

This is an example of how God leads us in praying about our past. What has surfaced as past events, wounds, choices that you may need to invite Christ into for healing?

As you begin to give these past wounds and events over to Jesus you'll notice over the months ahead how he'll take you back to those past seasons and address the heart issues that were overlooked at the time, or mishandled. I tell the story of a young friend's reaction to my new truck and . . . how God showed up.

A few weeks ago I bought a diesel pickup. I'm forty-six, but it was the first time I'd ever bought a car because I wanted to, because I liked it, not because the family needed it. A pickup does something for a man that a minivan just can't touch. Anyway, a young gal that works for us was riding along with me to go check on our horses. As she climbed into my truck, she was wowed. She loved it, exclaimed, "I had no idea the interior was like this!" And then, as I fired up the engine, she sighed and said, "I love the sound of a diesel engine."

I felt like The Man.

Now this had nothing to do with the beginnings of an affair. It had everything to do with the past. When I was fifteen, on one of those reckless party-filled Saturday nights, a few buddies and I took my parents' car out joyriding. I got caught, and my folks' reaction was to lay down an edict—I would not get my driver's license until I was eighteen. It wasn't a discipline; it was a punishment. It was over the top. No car, no driving through high school. It was *emasculating*. If I wanted to go see a girl, I had to ride my bike to her house. What a nerd. If I wanted to go on a date, she had to drive. What a little boy. I had to bum a ride to school every day from a friend. What a weenie. I never saw how emasculating this was until today.

Here I'd finally bought a pretty cool truck for myself, with my own cash, and I had this cute girl going nuts over it. It was a new experience. What caught my attention was this thought, or emotion, that leapt up from my heart: *I'm not the idiot.* Wow. How long had that been lying down there? Thirty-two years. Ever since high school (pages 157–158).

Healing the past involves both repentance and healing. Sometimes what we need to do is confess old sins, break old agreements, renounce old choices. But there is more. We also need to invite Christ's healing into these places. Invite Christ into those long-ago events, times, relationships, and wounds and he'll begin the healing process so needed, so wanted.

Will you invite him in? He longs to heal your past.

Clarity

I wrote *Walking with God* as "real-time entries" in order to show you how this all takes place as we move through our days. Far more often than not, issues in me that need inner healing just sort of present themselves. I don't usually go looking for them. They sort of find me. Usually through unwelcome emotions (I'm scared about a party or a meeting) or some old memory shows up (like never having a car) and that is the moment where we choose to walk with God. Don't blow past it—invite Christ in. Listen. Follow the trail.

Now, I do have a few friends who take the occasion of the passing of the year to do some reflecting. They'll get out their personal or family calendar and look back, assess. And I do find it worthwhile to stop and ask myself, *What do I want this year to be like? What do I want to change?*—that sort of thing. All that can be very healthy (page 160).

Have you ever done this? Has it been helpful?

New Year's might be an obvious time to ask the question, "What do I want this year to be like? What do I want to change? But you could ask it now. I mean—why wait? How would you answer it now?

The other issue here worth pausing over is asking God what he wants the theme of this season in your life to be about. I'll do this over certain events—Lord, what is this about? And I'll do it sometimes over seasons of my life.

> But I was asking God this morning what his word for the new year was, if he wanted to say anything about that, set a sort of theme for this year, and much to my surprise, I immediately heard, *Intimacy.* Almost before I finished asking the question. *Intimacy* between God and me. Yes. That sounds really good. Intimacy would be a shift, and a welcome one. A shift away from "Attack the day" and "Get things done" and even the nobler "Endure."
>
> Maybe it's even at the heart of the life I want to live, the source out of which all else flows (page 161).

What is Jesus saying to you about this season in your life?

NOT EVERY GOSPEL IS EQUAL

What did you think about this entry?

The key point of this story is: *not all gospels are equal*, we must make distinctions because much is at stake. Are you uncomfortable making distinctions between various movements in Christianity, or churches, or Christians? What do you fear about making distinctions?

talking about the length of Jesus' robe or how many angels can dance on the head of a pin here. What you believe about these issues will profoundly shape the rest of your Christian experience. My friend—who is somewhat loyal to the school—was really upset. "It's not right to say that," she said. "It's arrogant." Now, there is no question that it *could* be said arrogantly, but I wasn't being arrogant at all. I was making an observation, explaining why I don't want to refer people to this college (page 162).

What do you think—is it right or wrong to make observations like that? And voice them?

Wow. Paul is pretty hacked off here, and pretty vocal about what he sees. Now, you probably know the story—the Galatians had begun to embrace a gospel which said, "Yes, faith in Jesus Christ. We believe in Jesus Christ. *And,* you need to be circumcised, and keep the Law of Moses as well." A different gospel from the one that Jesus and Paul preached. A "sort-of" gospel. Just enough "Jesus" in there to make it *sound* like the real deal. But it's got other ideas and rules in it that are going to take these folks away from the heart of God and the relationship he offers. (There's a good bit of this still going around, by the way). It's a matter of profound concern and Paul isn't going to ignore it. This letter is a public document, which would have been read aloud not just in one church, but probably many. Paul has no problem saying, "Hey, wait a minute! You're wrong about this!" and doing so publicly (page 165–166).

There is a lot of this "Jesus and" in modern Christianity. The bottom line, the quick test, is always "You shall know them by their fruit." Thinking about the Christianity you or your loved ones live in, here are a couple of core questions:

🌿 Does it draw people into a true intimacy with God? As its main purpose?

🌿 Does it see wholeness and holiness as hand-in-hand, and, does it help people get there?

🌿 Does it take spiritual warfare seriously, and teach people to fight it?

This idea that both my friends were under—that it's wrong to draw distinctions and make value judgments between various forms of Christianity—this is not helpful. And it's not biblical. But it's got a lot of good people trapped in bad churches and programs. There's just enough Jesus words in there to make it *sound* like Christianity. But it's not the gospel Jesus preached. Not all gospels are equal. You must draw these distinctions. Don't just stay with the old gang because it's the old gang. Your loyalty is not to a church or a movement, but to Jesus Christ (pages 166–167).

What changes might be in order so that you find a fellowship living in the gospel Jesus preached?

What would keep you from making those changes?

Have you asked God about it? What is he saying?

A Sanctified Home

The point of this story is not to creep you out over some weird knife thing, get you worried about the things in your home. The point of the story is that we want to have our homes sanctified to Jesus Christ, just as we want

Brent said that dealing with foul spirits is like dealing with IRS agents—they are students of the law, and they know every technical twist and turn of the code. In the case of foul spirits, we've found that quite often you have to name them and bring the work of Christ against them specifically, or they won't leave. Remember—these are fallen, twisted, *disobedient* spirits—their very nature is to defy. Half asleep and half afraid, I was struggling to dial in enough to the Spirit of God to know exactly what I was dealing with and therefore pray effectively. It took some time, maybe fifteen minutes of continual prayer, bringing the work of Christ against fear (I knew at least fear was in the room) "and every dark thing," and sending them to the throne of Jesus Christ. Then I went back to sleep.

The next morning I remembered that I was still awake at midnight when the boys got home from a party, and then it dawned on me that I sensed something come into the house with them. It was a shadow, like when a cloud passes over the sun for a moment. But it was pitch dark in the house when I sensed something darker pass over or through or come in. Why didn't I pray right then? What is it in us that just doesn't want to deal with this stuff? We'd rather roll over, fluff our pillow, and hope it goes away. Well, this one didn't (pages 167–168).

🌾 When your warfare prayers don't seem to "work" is your tendency to do a little "*detective*" work or to simply give in?

🌾 And what has been the fruit of that?

Now, I'm not suggesting paranoia. Lots of stuff is benign. But when warfare hits, be a detective. *Is there a conduit? Where did this thing come from? Who did it belong to?* Pray over it; ask God what he thinks. It will prove to be very helpful.

. . . Now, there is no hard and fast law here. You have to follow the Spirit of God and ascertain the spirit of the article in question. Some things can be cleansed and sanctified to God.

Other things are better simply thrown out, or burned to ash in the Kidron Valley. And you may discover that you can have a conduit in your possession for some time and it doesn't seem to be a channel for evil, but then the enemy comes looking for an open door and finds this object useful to his purposes and it suddenly becomes a problem. The same principle holds true for unconfessed sins in our past or old agreements we have never

need to be sanctified and kept holy as well (pages 172–174).

What conduits might there be in your life, your home, your surroundings? What must you do?

Spring

A Time of Resurrection, Recovered Hope and Desire, a Time of New Beginnings

ACCEPTING WHAT I FIND
HARD TO ACCEPT

Okay—you might think me a little unstable, to be so affected by weather. But what affects your moods? Have you noticed? Can you name it? What sends you into a funk?

What do you do when it dawns on you that you're in one of your funks? Is there a better way to deal with these mood swings?

"To love winter, or to love anything or anybody, you must let go and give yourself over to it."

Which is a really good thing for those who have to live with me, 'cause it isn't any fun to live with a groundhog who's moping around the house, constantly griping about the weather (or anything else for that matter). I remember something Dennis Prager said—that "happiness is a moral obligation." The reason we are morally obligated to be happy is because people have to live with us. If I'm chronically unhappy, or even unhappy for more than a day or two, they pay for it. Do you want to live with Eeyore? Puddleglum? What's it like for the rest of the family when I'm frumping around the house? My unhappiness casts a long shadow. It's not fair to ask them to live under that.

Unhappiness is self-indulgent. It's like insisting everyone else listen to your taste in music. And it happens to be fugues, played on the organ (pages 176–177).

Have you ever before considered your unhappiness as self-indulgent?

What is God asking you to give yourself over to, in order to accept what you find hard to accept, and in order to love?

ON THE THINGS GOD WITHHOLDS

The weather got me thinking about acceptance and surrender. Which then led me to think about more significant, lingering, and long-standing disappointments in my life. I know you have yours too. What do we make of these things? How do we walk with God in them?

Now, I want to be careful here. There are many reasons for our losses and our unmet desires. The war we live in is reason enough. There *is* a thief, with a whole army behind him, and they steal, kill, and destroy like terrorists. When life isn't good we have to be careful we don't jump to the conclusion, "God is withholding this from me." We jump to it too quickly, as if the only cause and effect relationship in this world is God giving or not giving things to us. (Remember A+B=C? It's not how things work.) People can withhold love and kindness, even though God commands them not to. Is it God's fault? And frankly, we sabotage a lot of God's intended joy simply because of the way we approach our life (page 177).

Pause here. How do you think about the disappointments in your life—especially the long-standing ones? Why do they come? Why aren't they resolved?

It's really important we don't just jump to, or first jump to the conclusion, "God is holding out on me." There is the war, and there is sin, and this is a broken world. And many of us haven't really begun to walk with God in the sense of following him closely in the decisions of

The main point of this story is simply, there is no greater disaster for the human heart than this—to come to believe we have found life *apart* from God. And whatever might be the reasons for our disappointments, there is no question that God uses them to draw us to himself. To wean our hearts from every other perceived source of life, so that we might come to find our life in him. It takes a profound honesty and vulnerability to admit that the root of *some* of our most pronounced disappointments is our belief that God's love and God's life are *not* enough.

Isn't this what Adam and Eve were seduced into believing? That God was not enough? He had given them *so* much, but all they could see in that fateful moment was the one thing they *didn't* have. So they reached for it, even if it meant turning from God.

There is something we start out longing for, and the more we come to believe this is what we *have* to have in order to be happy, the more we obsess about it. The prize just out of reach swells far beyond its actual meaning. It begins to take on mythic proportions. We're certain life will come together once we achieve it. We think, *If only I was married. If only we had children. If only I was rich. If only I had*—fill in the blank. Everything else in our life pales in comparison. Even God. We are falling to believe we *need* whatever is just beyond our reach, and when we fall to this, we are miserable (page 178).

What is this for you? What do you think you *need?*

I am not minimizing the sorrow of our disappointments. The ache is real. What I am saying is that the ache swells beyond its nature, dominates the landscape of our psyche when we shift from, *How I long for this,* to, *I need this.* For the only thing we truly need is God, and the life he gives us. There is a satisfaction we don't want to come to until we come to it in God. Isn't this the satisfaction warned of in the parable of the barns (pages 178–179)?

In all of this I've found that God uses our disappointments and aches to turn us from everything else we grasp for back to the true source of life . . .

himself. React to my statement, *"For the only thing we truly need is God, and the life he gives us."*

This may be why every one of us bears at least one major and

Everyone has a cross to bear. Everyone. It reminds us every day that we cannot make life work the way we want. We can't arrive. Not completely. Not yet. If we'll let it, the disappointment can be God's way of continually drawing us back to himself.

I know that I face a choice. I can feel it down inside, I watch it take place in my heart. I can let my disappointments define my life. Or I can let them take me back to God, to find my life in him in ways I have not yet learned. The rest remains a mystery. But this is enough to know (page 180).

We all bear a cross. It is hard to accept . . . and oh, so necessary to see God in the disappointments of life. What do you suspect is *that thing that God seems to be withholding* that you bear and brings you back to God? And have you seen that it does bring you back to Him? And if it hasn't yet brought you back to him, why?

Can you break the agreement(s) that you've made regarding what you *need*? Give this place in your heart back to God. Ask him to fill you with his love and life, in this very place.

UNMET LONGINGS

In the course of a year how many times does God use a song, a movie, another person's life or story, a book or some life event to surface some longing of our heart he wants to address? A good part of this last year God has been raising and ministering to my longings and unmet desires. This is such an important issue to look at, for if we mishandle these unmet longings it sets us up for all types of addictions and idolatry, and unbelief. As you read this section what struck you most?

Why does God do this—stir up our longings?

I think what I do (and I see it in others) is simply bury them. And on one hand, of course we do. We have to. You cannot live your life with a constant awareness of heightened desires that are unmet, just as you can't go through your day continually pining for a life you do not have. You have to live the life you do have

with life." Which are you? And why?

To bury the deep longings of our hearts is not a good thing. It begins to shut our hearts down, and then we just fall into that "get on with life" mentality. For me, it means bearing down and working. Getting things done. But my passion slowly fades away, and life recedes from me. I cannot bring to my work the zest I once did, so even my work suffers. Because my heart is suffering. It's like a form of slow starvation. If your body doesn't get what it needs, you can run for awhile without it. But slowly the erosion begins to manifest itself. You're tired, your muscles ache, or you start having headaches or a thousand other symptoms. You need nourishment (page 181).

How does the ache of these unmet longings affect the way you live? I confessed how I just "bear down" and my heart slowly erodes. How do unmet longings affect your life?

Thank God, we cannot force it down forever. Hurting, it begins to insist on some attention. Now, we can either listen to those rumblings and let our hearts surface so that we bring them to God, or, this is where our addictions get in. The starving heart won't be ignored forever. Some promise of life comes along and boom—we find ourselves in the kitchen closet taking down a quart of ice cream, or cruising the internet for some intimacy (pages 181–182).

What addictions or "false comforters" are pulling at your heart these days? Can you see your longing for God in them?

God knows the danger of ignoring our hearts, and so he reawakens desire. You see a photo in a magazine, and pause, and sigh. You see someone with a life that reminds you of the life you once thought you would live. You're channel surfing one night and see someone doing the very thing you always dreamed you

desire, to stir our hearts up from the depths which we sent them to. He does it so that we don't continue to kill our hearts, and he does it so that we don't fall prey to some substitute that looks like life but will become an addiction in short order.

He sometimes does it so that we will seek the life we were meant to seek (page 182).

I share how I've buried my desire for friendship and intimacy. Yet God continues to stir up those yearnings. What have you found yourself saying, "*I want that too*" to?

I'm stunned by this whole process. The willingness and what feels like such a risk for God to reawaken desire in me. I mean, geez—to feel again a desire I've long buried. Yikes. I might make a wrong move, come to the wrong conclusion. Our friend might decide that what she really needs is a different spouse.

Something I read years ago by C.S. Lewis (in *The Weight of Glory*) has proven helpful to me time and time again, and may just rescue us in the very moment of awakened desire I am describing. Lewis is trying to show us that what God uses to awaken desire is *not* necessarily what we long for. The things "in which we thought the beauty was located will betray us if we trust to them; it was not *in* them, it only came *through* them, and what came through them was longing. These things . . . are good images of what we desire; but if they are mistaken for the thing itself, they turn into dumb idols, breaking the hearts of their worshippers. For they are not the thing itself . . ." They are not what we are longing for (pages 183–184).

What have you mistaken for your desire that was an image of what you really desire?

It's too late to become a professional baseball player or musician. Too late to have a child. This is the real danger zone, because it seems like there is no other choice but to put away this part of our heart. But to send your heart into exile because your longings have no hope of being met is to also exile your heart from the love of God. And he would have our whole heart. I'm no expert in this. It's hard to tell whether God is arousing some desire so that we might seek a new life, or simply so that this part of our heart might be made whole in him. But I have found that whatever else might be the case, we have to begin by giving this

So, as you ponder some of the deep desires of your heart what do you do with them? Do you put them in the category that *it's too late* to realize them or do you think God would have you pursue them in some fashion?

This really would be something to ask God about specifically. Take each desire to him and ask him what to do with each one . . . what does he have for you in *that* desire?

Over the course of this book I am hoping to show you the categories I find are essential to a daily walk with God. The issue of desire is central because what we do with desire is in many ways what we do with our hearts. How we handle desire is how we handle our hearts. There is so much more to say on the subject, and much of that is contained in another book of mine, *Desire*. You might find it helpful.

RESTING

This is a simple story of having asked God about a busy week beforehand—and as a result turning to some deeply needed rest I would not have turned to had I not asked. What strikes you about this story?

What level of pressure and stress, busyness and distraction do you live with on a daily basis—and just accept as inevitable?

✺ Does seeking God's counsel on your time and schedule come easy for you? Especially as you face those particularly stressful days and weeks? If not, why not?

The other "big idea" in this simple entry is that our walk with God will disrupt others, because most folks don't walk with God.

> I know I've disrupted a few people who did not take time for their hearts, disrupted their assumptions to take on the week just as I would have, had I not asked God. I don't know if they asked for advance words or not, or heeded what they heard. But it's disrupting to walk with God. And inviting too (pages 185–186).

✺ Whose life do you suspect your walk with God has disrupted? Why?

Are you reluctant to walk with God because it is disruptive?

How would you hope your life is inviting to others?

What upcoming events or circumstances do you want to take to God now?

SORTING THINGS OUT

As I said at the start of this book, life will present us with a hundred opportunities in a single week to take a look at our internal world, to walk with God there, to become more fully his.

Oh, how I wish I could underscore this lesson with trumpets and tympany and any other way to arrest your attention. This is huge. Don't let your internal life go unshepherded (page 189).

Where did you go with it, that is to say, what unfolded?

It was all I could do not to sulk.

I know my boys are teenagers now. I know they are developing lives of their own. But still . . . I was hurt. Disappointed. And something like lonely. Still am, as I come into my office to try and sort this out. I need to sort this out. (Don't just let your internal world roll on unrecognized and unshepherded.) Part of me wanted to let them know I was hurt (and defensive) right away. "Fine. I'll ask one of the guys. I know *they* want to go." *You little twerps. I mean, geez—think of all the young men*

out there who are dying for someone to take them anywhere. You
ingrates just don't know what you are turning down (page 186).

Where did your initial response take you? (Anger, shame, withdrawal, sulk, control . . . to one of your addictions?)

As I began to sort things out, God shepherded my heart to some very helpful insights. Ask Jesus what he is trying to show you through recent issues.

I'll include my prayer in hopes that it will help you journal out your prayer to God.

What is it that I need in this moment, God? I do know this—I know I need You to come and minister to me here. Jesus come, and meet me here, in this disappointment and hurt that I am feeling. I wanted them to be excited. I want them to see time with me as a highlight. It hurts to have my sons grow up and begin to pull away. It hurts to be dismissed for stuff like Xbox and movies and girlfriends. Meet me here.

I also know this—I know I don't want to punish them for not choosing me. Jesus, help me to love them even when they turn me down. Help me to love them and value them even when they take up hobbies and interests quite different from mine. Help me to love them as they pull away.

And now, at the end of all this journaling, my thoughts turn to You as my Father. I am embarrassed and pained to think how true all that I've just penned could be said of me towards you. That is,

We need God's help in sorting things out. And he will. Many times he chooses to change us rather than alter the difficult people and circumstances that provoke so much in us. How have you changed despite unchanging difficulties?

What did this story stir up in you?

Assault

⟫ What did this entry raise in you, what's your initial reaction?

All these stories and entries remind us that a year of life is a broad spectrum of emotions, battles, joys, triumphs, and struggles. That's life. The beauty and hope of our faith is that God is at work in *all* these things to bring us into an intimate relationship with him. That's the major theme—life and intimacy with God. HOWEVER, we must remember that we live in a world at war. Satan is also at work in many of the same events, acting as an opportunist, scheming ways to assault our heart.

I offered this story to illustrate three issues about warfare:

a) The enemy probes our perimeter, looking for a weakness or an opportunity, hoping to secure an agreement of some sort so that he can gain a hold and assault us even more. This probing is VERY common during those times when we are about something important for God and his kingdom.

b) When we come under an assault, it often clouds our judgment and our ability to discern what's going on. You shall know them by their fruits—confusion and haze are not from God.

c) We must admit our part in the whole mess, confess and renounce it, so that we can then banish the enemy. This DOESN'T mean every assault involves some sin on our part. But there may be, and if so it's crucial to take responsibility so that we can get victory over our enemy.

focused on the event, stay true, honor my colleagues, walk with God. But this stuff is coming on strong.

It felt as though the enemy were probing the perimeter, looking for a weakness. Lust. Then arrogance. Now distraction. Again and again. I think the conference gave me enough to concentrate on to maintain focus, sort of like driving in a rainstorm. You bear down, double your concentration, grip the wheel. But afterward I felt like crap. After holding off what the enemy had thrown at me, I felt like he then sent the big boys. A deep distress now entered in. Judgment galore. None of this is taking a verbal form, but the overwhelming sense is, *Look at you. You call yourself a man of God. You are utterly corrupt inside. And God is now far away* (pages 189–190).

The warfare against us may come in waves, as the enemy probes then exploits any weakness we have or door we leave open. What "probing" can you recognize of late?

It is so hard at these times to sort out what is really going on. What is genuine conviction, and what is assault? What is my fault and what is warfare? And where is the warfare coming from? Start with this—you shall know them by their fruits. Genuine conviction brings repentance. But not judgment, not contempt. Genuine conviction brings us back to God. It doesn't say to us, *You've blown it so bad he's removed himself from you.* I have to start with the fruit of this—I am deeply distressed. I feel anguish. I feel far from God. This is not from the Holy Spirit. Right now, that's about all I know.

In the smoke and fog of warfare it's easy to be confused over whether you're experiencing "conviction" or "assault." Have you been confused, or have you felt far from God over some event in the past several months?

I have to take responsibility for what part *is* mine. I opened the door to pride. I entertained it. I now see that the enemy was trying to penetrate my defenses by breaking down my integrity, any way he could. He found an agreement with pride. It came in when I saw how well things were going and the influence I was having and I let my heart go to, *You are really something.* So I confess and renounce the pride, the arrogance. I give God the glory for all that happened.

What are the sins that become doors to the enemy's exploits in your life?

It's so important to see that the assault isn't so much to get you to sin, but to separate you from God and leave you in a vicious cycle of self-contempt and shame that we assume to be the normal Christian life.

I have got to remember this—the issue is never the presenting sin. The issue is the surrender, however subtle, of our hearts. The open door, the agreement. What follows is the enemy's real goal—our separation from God, and from our true selves. I think most Christians never see the battle. They think they want evil, and they embrace the contempt as conviction. Then they assume that, of course, God is going to be distant, and they live under all of that for years. "My heart is evil, I am such a wretch, of course God is distant." They think it's the Christian life (page 192).

⚜ It might be helpful (and revealing) to stop, and remind yourself what the Christian life is about. Write down here your answer to this question: "What is it that God wants for you as his son or daughter—what is your Christian experience supposed to look like, feel like?"

LENT

⚜ Setting something down, and taking something up often happen as we listen to God. We set down our busyness so that we can "take up" rest, or joy. We let go our approach to life so that we can find true life with God. We let go old religious ties and allegiances so that we can take up a genuine walk with God. Do you see the rhythm? What is Jesus asking you to set down these days, and what is he asking you to take up?

Take those as two questions to bring to God. "Lord, what would you have me give up these days?"

Lent has been an annual mile marker for me in years past. Last year God again used this forty-day period to speak into my life. Asking him what he would have me give up I heard *self.*

"What is the Self thing I am to give up, Lord?" *Obsession.* Okay, it's self-obsession. I know what this means—that hyper self-awareness thing I do. Giving it up sounds wonderful. And next to impossible. I continue to write, and listen. "Yes, Jesus. I adore you. Yes. How do I give up self-obsession?" *Looking to my love in you.* Wow. That makes so much sense to me. This is so right on with all that God has been saying and doing to try and get me to shift over to his love. "I do, I do, I do want to return to your love in me. Say more, Lord—how do I get there? What's that look like? What do I look to now (page 194)?"

It took a bit of time and pursuit to get the clarity I needed from the simple words he spoke to me. If you don't understand what God is saying or addressing do you ask for more clarity?

> I'm lingering here, quieting my own hunches about where this is headed, neither ignoring them nor letting them write the rest of the script. "Say more, Lord—how do I get there? What's that look like? What do I look to now?" What I mean by "look to now" is, if I'm not looking to his love in me, where *am* I looking? I have a pretty good idea but I want to hear his thoughts on it.
>
> *Your ability to stay on top of things.*
>
> Right. Busted. Caught with my hand in the cookie jar. I love it when God does that. It is a wonderful sort of nakedness, to have him name the very thing we are doing and trying to hide we're doing, or doing and not even knowing it because we've been doing it for so long it's become normal to us. This sort of conviction has no shame to it. I know that what he's named is *exactly* what I do—I have placed all my confidence on my ability to "get it done," "get it right," "stay on top of things." No wonder I feel like I'm "just barely" walking with God. "Forgive me," I write. "It's so utterly unfaithful, so godless and self-reliant (pages 195–196)."

Clarify

And so, once again but through a different door, God has come to speak to me about my basic approach to life. It's not because the previous times didn't result in meaningful transformation. Not at all. It's simply that more transformation is needed. This is so important to keep in mind. When God continues to "come after" something in your life, it's not because you are blowing it. It's simply that it's time for more work there. God comes

Now, to add to the beauty of the story, for the past couple mornings when I've sat down at the table to have a quick bowl of oatmeal, I've opened my Bible to read a bit, and both times it just opened to Psalm 41. Here is what I read:

> I said, "O LORD, have mercy on me,
> heal me, for I have sinned against you." (41:4)

Do you hear David's approach to God? He doesn't expect to get slammed. He doesn't just promise to repent and do better. He knows he's turned from God, and he knows what he needs is *healing* (page 196).

So . . . indeed I've sinned by placing my confidence in myself instead of God BUT ultimately is it repentance and recommitting to greater effort in trusting God or is it turning to God for healing that ultimately will change you?

᠕ Do you see it, so much of our sin is the result of deep woundedness and brokenness. This doesn't absolve us from confession and repentance, it simply points to an even deeper core need we have . . . to be healed. Where do you still need healing? Are you talking with God about it?

SEEKING GUIDANCE

᠕ The Moab story has several really good treasures in it for our walk with God. But before I underscore them, let me simply ask, what jumped out at you as you read through this story?

I'm trying to figure out whether or not we should go to Moab this year. And right now, it's not really clear.

I'm praying about it, trying to get some guidance. My first question is, *Do we fight for the trip, Lord—or just let it go this year?*
busyness. Remember—we need joy. Lots and lots of joy.

Pause. Isn't our first reaction, when life gets busy, to start lightening the load, dumping cargo overboard so we don't drown? The problem is, we can dump the wrong things overboard (pages 196–197).

What has your busyness and the pace of your life caused you to "dump" overboard, caused you to leave behind or not pursue or walk away from?

Did you ask God about it?

How many precious things do we just let go, give up, surrender, because it seems that life is too busy? Or because it's a hassle to fight through to make it happen? Or simply because we assume we know what's best or inevitable, and we don't even stop to ask God?

We need to stop and ask. *Especially* when it seems like giving up some joy is inevitable. He might not agree (page 198).

"We assume we know what's best" . . . how is that true for you? Where has that been true with you?

What does your heart need for life and joy?

My guess is that whatever you put down is something that *doesn't* come easy. Right? You, like me, will probably have to fight for it. How will you fight for your heart and joy?

You see, the pace of our life in this world creates a momentum to our lives. Like cars on a freeway. And the truth is, quite often God's desires for us to run *against* that prevailing current. *Get off at the next exit.* The guidance of God is sometimes going to seem

its kind. And how will we *really* feel about letting it go when it's late April and there's two feet of snow outside and we are going stir crazy (page 198)?

A basic issue of walking with God is being more and more settled on his knowing what's best . . . what's needed for your heart. This is especially difficult when his guidance is counterintuitive. And yet it's in those moments when his counsel cuts against the grain of what we think is best or what we want that most reveals our relationship with Christ. How are you following God in ways that have been counterintuitive?

Even now, I'm trying to see into the future to figure out what's best. I'm filling in the blanks. We all do that. We try to figure it out. It's not the same thing as walking with God. We simply don't see all that God sees. "My thoughts are not your thoughts" (Isaiah 55:8). He knows what's ahead. He knows what we need (page 198).

⚹ Okay, this is huge. I said toward the beginning of the book that of all the issues involved in learning to hear the voice of God, surrender may be the most essential. As we learn to surrender, we find we can hear him better, more quickly, more clearly. But "filling in the blanks," sort of assuming we know what he's going to say, this is not surrender. It's more of speculation. Do you see this? Is it operating as you try and listen?

I *am* asking, but the reception isn't super clear right now. I don't have a signal. So what I've done is write out the questions on a pad of paper, one at a time:

Do we fight for Moab this year?   Or let it go?

This way I can sit with the question before God, praying, listening specifically on one issue at a time without all the other evidence pro and con clouding my thoughts. One question at a time.

Without weighing all the facts back and forth in my mind. For I am *not* trying to figure it out. I'm trying to hear from God. There is a difference. "My thoughts are not your thoughts," remember?

Sometimes I'll let the pad of paper sit on my desk for a

Fight for it? Really? *Really.* Okay. Fight for it (pages 198–199).

I shared this because I wanted to assure you that even though I've practiced listening to God for years, there are times when it doesn't come easy. DON'T JUST QUIT. Try something else, like writing down your questions and then giving God some time to bring the clarity.

I have my first piece of guidance. We are supposed to fight for this joy. (And you *will* have to fight for joy, friends. Do remember that). But the puzzle isn't solved yet. The conversation doesn't end here. *When* we go is a big issue as well. I've got to ask about that, too, or I could charge ahead and be just as mistaken as not having asked about this at all. Don't just stop with the first question. Ask the *next* question (pages 199–200).

Ask the next question! Have you been remembering to do this?

Late April is a gamble with the weather. It's been chilly a few times when we've gone in April, but it's always been warm when we've gone in May. We want warm. May makes sense. But I don't see how we could possibly pull it off in May. (There I go again, trying to figure it out). So I write on the page,

April?   May?

I hear *April, 21–24*, which is the weekend we do have open for this. Okay. We're going to Moab and we're going in April. Something in me feels a little "out there" with where this is landing. I realize I'm going to need to trust God on this. Smile. Isn't that the point—that we trust God enough to follow him? That we live by faith? Isn't that what this whole thing is about? The Christian life is not the common sense life. Oswald Chambers said that the only explanation for a Christian's life *has* to be the existence of God. Otherwise, it makes no sense (page 200).

Are you comfortable with that? Willing to live a life that doesn't make sense apart from God? If not, why not?

Now, I am not encouraging a senseless approach to life. This doesn't mean you follow every thought that passes through your head. There is wisdom, and there is revelation. They go together, hand in hand. "I keep asking that the God of our ——————————————— give you the Spirit ———

lean toward revelation (just asking God for direct guidance), then you need to balance your approach with wisdom. If you lean toward a wisdom approach to life, you must deliberately and consciously include revelation. Ask God (pages 200–201).

🌿 Which side have you leaned toward over the years? And lately?

🌿 So, what do you need to do, in order to live with both wisdom and revelation?

Having said that, we need to admit that there is always risk when we encourage others to walk with God. People have done a lot of really stupid things in the name of following Jesus. For that reason there are folks in the church who don't want to encourage this sort of risk, this "walking with God." Over the centuries they've tried to eliminate the messiness of personal relationship with Jesus by instituting rules, programs, formulas, methods, procedures. It may have eliminated some of the goofy things that happen when people are encouraged to follow God for themselves. But it also eliminated the very intimacy God calls us to. Don't surrender this treasure of intimacy with God because it can get messy (pages 201–202).

You will be opposed as you seek to listen to God's voice. Not just by our enemy, but by "well-meaning" Christians who don't believe this is biblical. You might find Dallas Willard's book, *Hearing God,* helpful as you build not just your understanding but your conviction about this lost treasure of the Christian faith.

NEW BEGINNINGS

⬩ What did this story about the puppy stir in you?

Stasi's desire to get a puppy exposed my hesitancy to open myself up to love again. Where are you hesitating about being vulnerable these days when it comes to issues of hope, or love, or desire? I was reluctant to open myself up to the inevitable pain love brings. I was steeling myself against the future. By doing this do you see how I cut myself off from the life God has for me? How

Why don't you ask Jesus about that, right now. Listen.

Jesus? I asked in my heart. Just a simple question, meaning, *What do you think about this? What do you want to say? What are your thoughts on the matter?*

Slowly but surely I am choosing this as my first response to anything. If I don't, I'm stunned by how fast my heart can react to a conversation or event. In a nanosecond I can jump to conclusions, make agreements, dismiss people. We all do this. Then we just move on. But it can be dead wrong. We might be in a bad mood. We're certainly biased. And who knows what else is influencing us on any given day.

Jesus?

I find myself doing that a lot these days. It allows him to speak into the moment as it's happening. It gives God a chance to be part of the process. Rather than looking to him later, after the damage has been done.

Jesus?
It would be good (page 203).

I quickly turned to Jesus for his input on Stasi's desire for a puppy. As you've been going through this guidebook have you found yourself turning to Christ as a first response to most things?

How has that changed you or your life?

And what would keep you from doing this more often?

I believe Christianity is at its core a gospel of life. I believe great breakthrough and healing is available. I believe we can prevent the thief from ransacking our lives, if we will do as our Shepherd says. And when we can't seem to find the healing or the breakthrough, when the thief does manage to pillage, I believe ours is a gospel of resurrection. Whatever loss may come, that is not the end of the story. Jesus came that we may have life (page 204).

This may be one of the most important paragraphs in the whole book. Read it through again. Do you believe it?

RETURNING TO LOVE

I bought a new journal this week because my old one had filled up, and I have more time than usual to linger with God this morning before heading into the day. So, I pour myself a cup of coffee, sit down on the couch and pull out the journal. I always feel strange about writing on the first page of a new journal. I mean, here it is—a brand new journal. All those clean, white pages. Nothing yet has been set down. It feels . . . momentous. Kind of like a new beginning. Or at least, a new era. What will unfold? And what to put on page one? I always have this feeling that it needs to be significant. After all, this is the opening page of a new book in my life, the next chapter with God. It seems to deserve something weighty. Something transcendent.

Looking down at the blank page, I quietly ask God in my heart, *What needs to go here?*

You know what he said.

My love.

So that is what I write down. That is all I write on that opening page. Two words. My Love. It is more than enough. Whatever else gets written in this journal, whatever stories told, whatever prayers, all the processing of life, let it all come under this. Let it be a continuation of this. His love. And then I sit there and look at it. Let it sink in. Come back to it in my heart. I am turning my heart towards his love. Letting it be true. Letting it be life to me (pages 204–205).

Our journey is almost over. How will you continue to journal and listen and think about your life and your walk with God? What is your *plan*?

And what will your "new page" say on it? Ask Jesus about that, right now.

And something in me is shifting. I am coming to believe it more than I ever have before. It's changing me. I feel less driven. Less compulsive. Less grasping. And less empty. I feel like I want to live. I'll live in this hope (page 205).

Take a few moments now to reflect on what you've learned after reading the book and doing this study. Think about what especially stood out to you.

> As I explained in the introduction, what I have attempted in these pages was to faithfully record what a year's experience of walking with God looks like. Feels like. Sounds like. As I read back over my words, they seem true to what has happened. And yet, so very incomplete. There are hundreds more stories I could have told, had I room to tell them. A lot goes on in a year of our lives, doesn't it? I don't want to leave a wrong impression— these stories are a sampling, offered in hopes of shedding light on your own story, helping you learn to hear the voice of God and walk with him whatever may come your way. I hope they have at least been alluring—this sort of relationship with God is available. To us all. My greater hope is that these stories have been instructive, and you are finding this walk yourself (*Walking with God*, page 207).

⚛ Well—what is your overall reaction? Has it been alluring? Instructive? Explain.

⚛ What is changing in your life as a result of having walked through this?

> May I strongly suggest reading through this book again—I know I'm always amazed how much more I get out of a book on a second reading. . . . What a wonderful idea it would be to take your time and dive even more deeply into these themes, maybe do so with a few friends. For as I also said in the introduction, learning to walk with God is our deepest need. Everything else in your life depends on it. Don't let anything hold you back from this great treasure (page 208).

⚛ DON'T JUST WALK AWAY! Don't just move on to the next distraction. How will you continue in this? Start a small group? Read it again yourself? Be specific.

(Do drop by the Ransomed Heart website at RansomedHeart.com/ WalkingwithGod and watch Video 18 for more on this topic. There is so much more for you there.)

Several months have passed since I turned in this manuscript. Many more stories have unfolded. . . . My sleep has been good and then not so good. There has been a great deal more healing of my past. . . . God has been guiding my reading of Scripture,

it). This convelsu

my every day. I cannot even begin to say how thankful I am for it (page 208).

What is your prayer to God at this point? Write it below.

Now, take a few moments to reflect on the past year and the season of life you are in.

I structured this book around the four annual seasons of a year for literary reasons (I found it beautiful) and also because I found—looking back—that the seasons somehow captured, or paralleled, the very things Jesus was doing in my life at the time. (Summer as a period of richness; fall a time of trial; winter the season of "letting go"; spring a time of new hope and of renewal.) For our walk with God does have thematic elements to it; he seems to be "up to something" specific during certain episodes of our lives.

It can prove immensely helpful, therefore, to ask God to help you see what he is wanting to accomplish in you during a particular episode, or season, whether that be a new school year, a job change, a move to a new church or a new part of the world. What are you up to here, Lord—in this? is a very helpful question to ask (page 209).

As you look back on the year, how have the seasons captured what Jesus has been doing in your life? What has God been "up to" during these times?

Every New Year, around the first week of January, I spend some quiet moments asking Jesus what he has to say about the year before us. These are not so much words of guidance or warning as much as they prove to be "themes" of the year, words that capture the essence of broad patterns or lessons the year will hold. . . .

God has themes for each us not only for the seasons of a year but also for the larger seasons of life. The more we can come to understand what those seasons are—and the themes for them— the better we can align ourselves with what God is up to, the better we can walk with him (page 210).

What are some ways you are seeking to align yourself with what God is doing right now in your life?

Letting Go

Each of us are in a different season of life. For me, as I explain in the book, I ~~am in the~~ "empty nest" season. And with that season has come some changes.

and what to do when y...

How much can you—and should you—weigh in on their decisions about issues such as when to have children and when and how to parent those children? Oh my. Now that we are neck-deep in it, I find this season to be much harder than parenting younger children. And how desperately we need to walk with God in it.

Hang on now—I know our days are not as crowded with carpool and sports and homework and the madness of a household in the younger-children years. We can eat cereal for dinner if we want; we get to go to bed when we want; we aren't constantly tripping over dirty soccer shoes or picking Play-Doh out of the carpet. The empty nest years can look like easier years, and maybe they are in some respects. But the consequences of children's choices grow far more staggering as they get older. The stakes are much higher (pages 210–211).

As you look back on the past five years, what major changes have you made? How are the stakes "higher" for you today than they were five years ago?

You Must Grieve Their Leaving

A book on parenting adult children is a book I cannot write because I would need to unveil how we are navigating our children's choices. And their choices as adults are not mine to disclose to the public. Plus, we are still in the thick of it, and I don't want to reveal all my game plans to them either. But here are a few things I wish we had been told. . . .

We've done it three times now, and it never got any easier—dropping off our sons for college, out of state, and just driving away. You say good-bye, and you drive away. The pain of this was incomparable to just about anything we had yet experienced as parents, largely because it was such a symbolic event. Our family life would never, ever be the same. The childhood years were over. That season was closed. Forever. One by one their bedroom lights were turned off and a massive black hole opened up in the family. Instead of nightly dinner conversations, we would only hear from them when they wanted to talk—which in the college years turned out to be mostly when they needed money. Our relationship with them would never, ever be the same.

The pain of saying good-bye was excruciating. What surprised us was the anger we felt (pages 211–212).

Pause here. What seasons are now closed for you? How have you responded to those losses?

to want to ask Jesus to interpret. Too many [ ] off to fill the void with activity and miss the season they are in with God. In missing that, they miss so much else.

Which brings me back to walking with God through the seasons of life. Where are we now, Lord? What are you up to? How do I interpret this? What are you saying over it (page 213)?

Take a moment to write a prayer below, asking Jesus these questions.

THE STAGES OF LIFE

I hesitate to be so presumptuous as to name the larger stages of human life, knowing how varied all our individual experiences are. But I think the examples will help more than harm given the ground we have covered together in this book. For I trust that you will check in with Jesus to know how to apply anything here to your own life (page 212).

🌿 Read the descriptions of the stages of life on pages 213–216. What is a key lesson you have learned from a stage of life you have recently gone through?

🌿 What is a key lesson you have learned from a stage of life you have recently gone through?

What Matters More

As we mature in our life with God, he allows us to participate more deeply in the things he is doing on earth. He invites us to take larger roles in his mission. Quite often it coincides with him entrusting to us the very desires of our own hearts, which in a less mature stage we could not be given the keys to. We quit our career and join a youth mission; we devote our empty nest free time to rescuing young girls from the sex trade; we volunteer doing something we love and care about. It can be incredibly fulfilling. It opens up a whole new walk with God—being on mission with him (page 216).

Relate this to your own life. How has God invited you to participate in the things he is doing on earth? How you have acted on those things?

is activity for God, and that is very, very
with God. And so God asks us to let it go (pages 216–217).

Have you seen this in your life? What is God asking you to let go?

"ALLOW THINGS TO CHANGE"

Our treasured memories of those summer trips [in days gone by] are filled with ice-cream cones and swimming spots and evening canoe trips and bedtime prayers. But now I needed to allow for the fact that our children's marriages require their own time and space, and so we didn't always do the evening canoe trip as a family. Furthermore, Stasi and I wanted to go to bed by nine, just around the time the young adults were ready to go out for some nightlife. All sorts of joy took place, and we only heard about it. And so each day I found treasured traditions disrupted by new desires and changing needs, and again and again I needed to come back to, Allow things to change. As I did, I found my heart free to let go, free not to insist on things being a certain way, free to love with an open hand and open expectations. I'd really rather live that way (page 218).

≈ And now we are at the end of our journey together. What are some things that God is telling you to *allow to change*? How are you feeling about these coming changes?

Over the years I have grown in my understanding of prayer and spiritual warfare and of our need to be restored in the life of God each day. And so I have developed this prayer, which I call "The Daily Prayer." I call it that because I pray it daily. Before anything else. Even breakfast. The prayer has morphed through several versions as I've learned something new about the work of Christ for us or the ploys of the enemy. And so I offer you this, the latest version. May it be a source of life to you. Daily.

THE DAILY PRAYER

My dear Lord Jesus, I come to you now to be restored in you, to be renewed in you, to receive your love and your life and all the grace and mercy I so desperately need this day. I honor you as my Sovereign, and I surrender every aspect of my life totally and completely to you. I give you my spirit, soul, and body, my heart, mind, and will. I cover myself with your blood—my spirit, soul, and body, my heart, mind, and will. I ask your Holy Spirit to restore me in you, renew me in you, and to lead me in this time of prayer. In all that I now pray, I stand in total agreement with your Spirit and with my intercessors and allies, by your Spirit alone.

[Now, if you are a husband, you'll want to include your wife in this time of prayer. If you are a parent, you'll want to include your children. If this doesn't apply to you, jump to the paragraph following this one.]

In all that I now pray, I include (wife and/or children, by name). Acting as their head, I bring them under your authority and covering, as I come under your authority and covering. I cover (wife and/or children, by name) with your blood—their spirits, souls, and bodies, their hearts, minds, and wills. I ask your Spirit to restore them in you, renew them in you, and apply to them all that I now pray on their behalf, acting as their head.

Dear God, holy and victorious Trinity, you alone are worthy of all my worship, all my heart's devotion, all my praise, all my trust, and all the glory of my life. I love you, I worship you, I trust you. I give myself over to you in my heart's search for life. You alone are life, and you have become my life. I renounce all other gods and all idols, and I give you the place in my heart and in my life that you truly deserve. I confess here and now that this is all about you, God, and not about me. You are the hero of this story, and I belong to you. Forgive me for my every sin. Search me and know me and reveal to me where you are working in my life. Grant to me the grace of your healing and deliverance and a deep and true repentance.

Heavenly Father, thank you for loving me and choosing me before you made the world. You are my true Father—my Creator, my Redeemer, my Sustainer, and the true end of all things, including my life. I love you, I trust you, and I worship you. I give myself over to you to be one with you in all things, as Jesus is one with you. Thank you for proving your love by sending Jesus. I receive him and all his life and all his work, which you ordained for me. Thank you for including me in Christ, for for-

[illegible] for making

[illegible]

thanks and g[illegible]

body, my heart, mind, and will. I bring the life and the work of Jesus over [wife and/or children, by name] and over my home, my household, my vehicles, my finances—all my kingdom and domain.

Jesus, thank you for coming to ransom me with your own life. I love you, I worship you, I trust you. I give myself over to you, to be one with you in all things. And I receive all the work and all of the triumph of your cross, death, blood, and sacrifice for me, through which I am atoned for, I am ransomed and transferred to your kingdom, my sin nature is removed, my heart is circumcised unto God, and every claim made against me is disarmed this day. I now take my place in your cross and death, through which I have died with you to sin, to my flesh, to the world, and to the evil one. I take up the cross and crucify my flesh with all its pride, arrogance, unbelief, and idolatry (and anything else that is a current struggle). I put off the old man. I ask you to apply to me the fullness of your cross, death, blood, and sacrifice. I receive it with thanks and give it total claim to my spirit, soul, and body, my heart, mind, and will.

Jesus, I also sincerely receive you as my life, my holiness, and my strength, and I receive all the work and triumph of your resurrection, through which you have conquered sin, death, and judgment. Death has no mastery over you, nor does any foul thing. And I have been raised with you to a new life, to live your life—dead to sin and alive to God. I now take my place in your resurrection and in your life, through which I am saved by your life. I reign in life through your life. I receive your life—your humility, love, and forgiveness; your integrity in all things; your wisdom and discernment; your strength; your joy; and your union with the Father. Apply to me the fullness of your resurrection. I receive it with thanks and give it total claim to my spirit, soul, and body, my heart, mind, and will.

Jesus, I also sincerely receive you as my authority, rule, and dominion, my everlasting victory against Satan and his kingdom, and my authority to bring your kingdom at all times and in every way. I receive all the work and triumph of your ascension, through which you have judged Satan and cast him down, disarming his kingdom. All authority in heaven and on earth has been given to you, Jesus, and you are worthy to receive all glory and honor, power and dominion, now and forevermore. And I have been given fullness in you, in your authority. I now take my place in your ascension and in your throne, through which I have been raised with you to the right hand of the Father and established in your authority. I now bring the kingdom of God and the authority, rule, and dominion of Jesus Christ over my life today, over my home, my household, my vehicles and finances—over all my kingdom and domain.

I now bring the authority, rule, and dominion of the Lord

Jesus Christ and the fullness of the work of Christ against Satan, against his kingdom, and against every foul and unclean spirit that come against me. [At this point, you might want to name the spirits that you know have been attacking you.] I bring the

[text illegible due to blurring] ... foul power and black art.

[text illegible]

... you, I ...

victory in Pentecost, through which you have come. You have clothed me with power from on high and sealed me in Christ. You have become my union with the Father and the Son; the Spirit of truth in me; the life of God in me; and my Counselor, Comforter, Strength, and Guide. I honor you as my Sovereign, and I yield every dimension of my spirit, soul, and body, my heart, mind, and will to you and you alone, to be filled with you, to walk in step with you in all things. Fill me afresh. Restore my union with the Father and the Son. Lead me in all truth, anoint me for all of my life and walk and calling, and lead me deeper into Jesus today. I receive you with thanks, and I give you total claim to my life.

Heavenly Father, thank you for granting to me every spiritual blessing in the heavenlies in Christ Jesus. I claim the riches in Christ Jesus over my life today, my home, my kingdom and domain. I bring the blood of Christ over my spirit, soul, and body, my heart, mind, and will. I put on the full armor of God— the belt of truth, breastplate of righteousness, shoes of the gospel, helmet of salvation. I take up the shield of faith and sword of the

Spirit, and I choose to wield these weapons at all times in the power of God. I choose to pray at all times in the Spirit.

Thank you for your angels. I summon them in the authority of Jesus Christ and command them to destroy the kingdom of darkness throughout my kingdom and domain, destroy all that is raised against me, and establish your kingdom throughout my kingdom and domain. I ask you to send forth your Spirit to raise up prayer and intercession for me this day. I now call forth the kingdom of the Lord Jesus Christ throughout my home, my family, my kingdom, and my domain in the authority of the Lord Jesus Christ, with all glory and honor and thanks to him.

Thank you for your willingness to lead a group through Walking with God: How to Hear His Voice. During the lessons in this study, you will explore what it means to to have a relationship with God and how to follow his leading in every season. You will find the rewards of leading to be different from that of participating, and we hope you find your relationship with Jesus deepened by the experience. This leader's guide will give you some tips on how to prepare for your time together and faciliate a meaningful experience for your group members.

WHAT DOES IT TAKE TO LEAD THIS STUDY?

Get together and watch God show up. Seriously, that's the basics of how a small group works. Gather several people who have a hunger for God, will be open and honest with God and themselves, and who desire to have a closer walk with him. God will honor this every time and show up in the group. You don't have to be a pastor, priest, theologian, or counselor to lead a group through this study. Just invite people over, discuss the questions, and talk about it. All you need is a willing heart, a little courage, and God will do the rest. Really.

How This Study Works

Make sure everyone in your group has a copy of this study guide. It works best if you can get the guides to your group before the first meeting. That way, everyone can read the chapter you will be discussing ahead of time.

Each week, you'll meet together to discuss the material. This study is ideal for use in small groups, but it can also be used in classroom settings, such as Sunday school classes (though you may need to modify the discussion time depending on the size of the class). You could even use the material in this guide for a special prayer retreat.

NOTE: Due to the length of the Summer, Fall, Winter, and Spring chapters, you may not be able to get through all of the material in one session. For this reason, you may wish to break up the material in those chapters into two separate sessions ("part one" and "part two"). The following is one way in which you could do this, for a total of ten sessions:

Session	Title	Pages	Section(s)
1	Prelude	1–14	entire chapter
2	Summer (part one)	15–30	start—"What Should I Read?"
3	Summer (part two)	30–50	"What Should I Read?"—end
4	Fall (part one)	51–71	start—"The Next Day"
5	Fall (part two)	71–92	"The Next Day"—end
6	Winter (part one)	93–115	start—"The Power of the Right Word"
7	Winter (part two)	115–142	"The Power of the Right Word"—end
8	Spring (part one)	143–166	start—"Lent"
9	Spring (part two)	166–184	"Lent"—end
10	In Closing	185–196	entire chapter

Basically, each week you and your group will: (1) read the material covered in this guide (which corresponds to the chapters in the *Walking with God* trade book), (2) answer the questions found in this guide, and (3) talk about it. That's it!

A Few Tips for Leading a Group

The setting really matters. If you can choose to meet in a living room over a conference room in a church, do it. Pick an environment that's conducive to people relaxing and getting real. Remember the enemy likes to distract us when it comes to prayer and seeking God, so do what you can to remove these obstacles from your group (silence cell phones, limit background noise, no texting). Set the chairs or couches in a circle to prevent having a "classroom" feel.

Have some refreshments! Coffee and water will do; cookies and snacks are even better. People tend to be nervous when they join a new group, so if you can give them something to hold onto (like a warm mug of coffee), they will relax a lot more. It's human nature.

Be honest. Remember that your honesty will set the tone for your time together. Be willing to answer questions personally, as this will set the pace for the length of people's responses and will make others more comfortable in sharing.

Stick to the schedule. Strive to begin and end at the same time each week. The people in your group are busy, and if they can trust you to be a good steward of their time, they will be more willing to come back each week. Of course, you want to be open to the work God is doing in people as they learn new aspects of desire they might not have understood before, and at times you will want to linger in prayer. The clock serves you; your group doesn't serve the clock. But work to respect the group's time, especially when it comes to limiting the discussion times.

Don't be afraid of silence or emotion. Welcome awkward moments. Most people are nervous when it comes to talking about their spiritual life and the stumbles they have in their relationship with God. Ease into it. By week three or four you'll be humming along.

Don't dominate the conversation. Even though you are the leader, you are also a member of this small group. So don't steamroll over others in an attempt to lead—and don't let anyone else in the group do so either.

Prepare for your meeting. Review the material in this guide ahead of time, as this will better prepare you for what the session might stir in the hearts of your group members. Also spend some time in prayer. In fact, the most important thing you can do is simply pray ahead of time each week:

> *Lord Jesus, come and rule this time. Let your Spirit fill this place. Bring your kingdom here. Take us right to the things we really need to talk about and rescue us from every distraction. Show us the heart of the Father. Meet each person here. Give us your grace and love for one another. In your name I pray.*

Make sure your group members are prepared. Once again, make sure every person has a copy of this study guide before the first meeting. You might want to also send out a reminder email or a text a couple of days before the meeting to make sure folks don't forget about it.

As You Gather

You will find the following counsel to be especially helpful when you meet for the first time as a group. I offer these comments in the spirit of "here is what I would do if I were leading a group through this study."

First, as the group gathers, start your time with introductions if people don't know each other. Begin with yourself and share your name, how long you've been a follower of Christ, if you have a spouse and/or children, and what intrigues you the most about this study. Going first will put the group more at ease.

After each person has introduced himself or herself, share—in no more than five minutes—what your hopes are for the group. Then jump into the discussion, as this will help get things started on a strong note. In the following weeks you will then want to start by allowing folks to catch up a little—say, fifteen minutes or so—with some "hey, so how are you?" kind of banter. Too much of this burns up your meeting time, but you have to allow some room for it because it helps build relationships among the group members.

Note that each group will have its own personality and dynamics. Typically, people will hold back the first week or two until they feel the group is "safe." Then they will begin to share. Again, don't let it throw you if your group seems a bit awkward at first. Of course, some people never want to talk, so you'll need to coax them out as time goes on. But let it go the first week.

Insight for Discussion

If the group members are in any way open to talking about their lives as it relates to this material, you will not have enough time for every question in this study guide—even if you break the longer chapters into two parts. That's okay! Pick the questions ahead of time that you know you want to cover, just in case you end up only having time to discuss a few of them.

You set the tone for the group. Your honesty and vulnerability during discussion times will tell them what they can share. How long you talk will give them an example of how long they should. So give some thought to what stories or insights from your own work in the study guide you want to highlight.

WARNING: The greatest temptation for most small group leaders is to add to the teaching with a little "teaching session" of their own. This is unhelpful for two reasons. First, you don't want your group members "teaching" or "lecturing" or "correcting" one another. Every person is at a different place in his or her spiritual journey—and that's good. But if you set a tone by teaching, the group will feel like they have the freedom to teach one another. That can be disastrous for group dynamics. Second, the participants will have read all of the material in this guide ahead of the session. They don't need more content! They want a chance to talk and process their own lives in light of all they have taken in.

A Strong Close

Some of the best learning times will take place after the group time as God brings new insights to the participants during the week. Encourage group members to write down any questions they have as they read through this guide and answer the questions. Make sure they know you are available for them, especially as they get deeper into the study. Finally, make sure you close your time by praying together. Perhaps ask two or three people to pray, inviting God to fill your group and lead each person during this study.

Thank you again for taking the time to lead your group. May God reward your efforts and dedication and make your time together fruitful in this study for his kingdom.

About the Authors

 John Eldredge is an author of numerous bestselling books, including *Wild at Heart*, *Fathered by God*, and *Beautiful Outlaw*. He is also director of Ransomed Heart, a ministry devoted to helping people discover the heart of God, recovering their own hearts in God's love, and learning to live in God's kingdom. John and his wife, Staci, live near Colorado Springs, Colorado.

 Craig McConnell was an integral part of the Ransomed Heart speaking team until he went to the Kingdom in 2016. He loved the beach, good music, and deep friendships. His teachings continue to transform lives and can be found at RansomedHeart.com.

RANSOMED HEART'S
FREE GIFT TO YOU

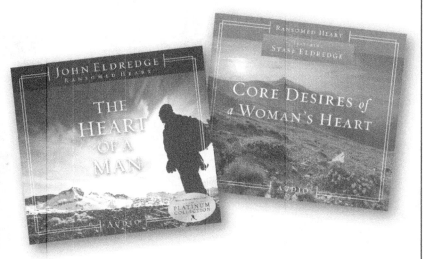

Recorded live, these powerful messages from John and Stasi
Eldredge speak to the core desires of the male and female
heart. Choose one or both full-length audio downloads.

Visit RansomedHeart.com, click to the Store page, and input the audio
title you want (*The Heart of a Man* and/or *Core Desires of a Woman's Heart*).
At checkout, type the code HEART and you will receive one or both
audio downloads at no charge.

LOVE GOD. LIVE FREE.

THERE IS SO MUCH MORE

When people think about Ransomed Heart, some connect it solely with John Eldredge's books—or perhaps with the live events in Colorado.

But there is so much more.

This 54-minute free download is the ideal resource for all who want to know more about the heart of Ransomed Heart Ministries.

Available exclusively at **RansomedHeart.com**.

RANSOMED HEART
LOVE GOD. LIVE FREE.